Delighted To Die

For the Joy Set Before Him

Don Atkin

Cover Design by Denise Douglas

Unless otherwise quoted, all Scripture quotations are from the Holy Bible, New King James Version (NKJV, copyright 1982 by Thomas Nelson, Inc.).

Scripture quotations marked TM are from the Message Bible by Eugene H. Peterson, copyright 2002, 2005. All rights reserved.

A Man Who Lived in View of Eternity

On March 9th, 1791, when John Wesley was carried to his grave, he left behind him a good library of books, a well-worn clergyman's gown, and a much abused reputation. But also, an England moved to the very depths and a Church thrilled through and through with an awakened spiritual life. John Wesley was a man who truly possessed both apostolic vision and gifts, but most importantly he was a man who lived in view of eternity. "Consumed by the thought of the shortness of time, the great work to be done, and the need for haste in doing it, on he marched, preaching, pleading, warning and guiding."

From Matthew Henry's Commentary on 2 Peter 1:

The nearness of death makes the apostle diligent in the business of life. Nothing can so give composure in the prospect, or in the hour, of death, as to know that we have faithfully and simply followed the Lord Jesus, and sought his glory.

Scared to Death of Death

Since the children are made of flesh and blood, it's logical that the Savior took on flesh and blood in order to rescue them by His death. By embracing death, taking it into Himself, He destroyed the Devil's hold on death and freed all who cower through life, scared to death of death.[1]

There is no bondage so binding as the fear of death. Its tentacles captivate every area of life, virtually paralyzing believers from fulfilling their potential.
– Don Atkin

[1] Hebrews 2:14-15 TM

Contents

Foreword

The Lamp

Rheba Drye

My mother, Nadine Smith, passed away in her sleep on April 20. Her old body of 96 years was worn to a frazzle. As she was drifting closer to death, my brothers and sister tiptoed into her room at Abingdon Assisted Living to quietly whisper their good-byes. Every one of the employees on duty that night heard that she was passing. They, too, joined my siblings to whisper their good-byes through their muffled tears. "I love you, Mrs. Nadine," they said. "We will miss you, Mrs. Nadine!"

I was not there when she passed. I had said my good-byes in February, when I visited her and helped my siblings celebrate her birthday. I remember her sitting in her wheelchair, her beautiful white head drooping to her right side. I drew close to her ear and asked, "Do you know who I am, Mother?" She raised her head and slowly replied, "No, I don't believe I do." I choked back the tears. For the first time in my 68 years of life, my mother didn't know me! I knew then that her physical and mental systems had taken a huge spiral downward since my last visit in December. I told my sister Phyllis, "I wonder if I will see her alive again." Before I left for Macon, I changed the contents of her shadow box (which held her name I had written in calligraphy) outside her door from winter to spring. I told Phyllis, "I think this is the last time I will change her shadow box."

We held her funeral at Mt. Holly Pentecostal Holiness Church, where I grew up and where Sam and I married. When people live to age 96, most of their friends have died, and there are few left to eulogize them. Not so with Mother. The church was packed with children, grandchildren, great-grandchildren, one great-great-grand-child, former employees with whom Mother worked, church members, neighbors and friends. Sam and two other ministers did the service. But there was no usual sermon, because **her life was the sermon**. One by one, her children and grandchildren told how deeply their lives had been touched by my mother. We shared the funny events, her spiritual impact, her prayers for us and the deeds she did for all of us through the years. I was struck by the fact that the bridge between the generations had been crossed so beautifully. A common thread bound us together: an ancient woman had touched us all, no matter what our ages. The story was told, not about a beautiful, flawless, energetic young person, but about a withered, wonderful, lovable Matriarch!

And then we laid her tired old body to rest where she is now buried beside my father who died when I was sixteen.

This week I went back to Gastonia to help my sister go through her belongings. We were amazed at the things she had saved through the years. I found my daddy's work log from 1929. She had saved a letter from Sam that dated twenty years back. (He quoted from the letter at the funeral.) There were no costly items that would bring big bucks on the Antiques Road Show, just simple things. I chose to keep her worn bread pan in which she baked her famous biscuits, a few of her watches and her purse. But the thing I most cherish is the lamp that sat on her nightstand by her bed in our old home place.

Ah, the lamp. The tears flowed yesterday as I lovingly cleaned it and put it in a special place in our bedroom. It has six brass feet, which remind me of Mother's six children whom she loved and prayed for, up until her last days on earth. The white ceramic base has tiny embossed flowers that remind me of the flowers of beauty that her life represented. I mused as I gently cleaned the lamp and shade, "I wonder how many people she prayed for over the years before she turned off this lamp every night?" All of her children and grandchildren, pastors, relatives, neighbors, wayward sons and daughters, missionaries, TV evangelists, Dave Wilkerson, whom she loved, supported and respected . . . how long would the list be?

Her light went out on April 20. But her lamp has not gone out, but burns brightly because she let her light pierce the hearts of all who chose to draw close to her, to honor her, to respect her, and draw from her storehouse of wisdom. The cord of her life was connected to her heavenly Source of strength and power.

I promise not to let my light dissipate, but to let it burn brighter so it will penetrate the hearts of others. I want to emulate your example, Mother, to pass a legacy to our son Jeff, daughter-in-law Brianne, granddaughter Julianna, and to all who come into my sphere of influence.

I will let the lamp be a reminder to pray for others, just like you. I say, "Good night, Mother." But you now say, "Good morning, Jesus!" [1]

---

[1] Rheba and her husband, Sam, have faced death several times. They lost two daughters, one in a car accident, and the other to a brain aneurism. Rheba battled breast cancer for many years. Sam has had numerous heart issues. With Jesus, they are "acquainted with grief." Through Him, they are "more than conquerors." By Him, they continue to bring life to others in many nations.

Preface

Woody Allen has said, "I'm not afraid of death. I just don't want to be there when it happens."

"Cute." And, he undoubtedly speaks for many people.

Not all believers have settled the issues concerning death. I am writing this because I want to help people (1) live prepared to die, and (2) prepare to live by dying to self.[1] These are keys to overcoming in life.

I am praying that we who follow Jesus fully will find the same grace to die that we find to live. The same Jesus who shows us how to live also shows us how to die:

The author and finisher of our faith, who ***for the joy that was set before Him*** *endured the cross, despising the shame, and has sat down at the right hand of the throne of God.*[2]

He gave His life *for the joy that was set before Him.* We are the joy that was set before Him!

---

[1] This is not our works. This is believing that we died when Christ died. We were buried with Him in baptism, and rose to walk in newness of life—new creatures with the Spirit of Christ within.

[2] Hebrews 12:2

Now, we get to give our lives *for the joy that is set before* us. *Jesus* is *the joy that is set before* us!

There is *a time to be born, and a time to die.*[3]

Dad is ninety-seven. He says, "I'm ready, but not in a hurry." A man at peace, He often speaks of waking up some morning in heaven.

But, what about the younger ones who face death by sickness or disease, or are snatched from this life by an untimely accident? God knows. I don't need to know. Methuselah lived nine hundred and sixty-nine years. A granddaughter's friend lost her little boy at the age of eight months when he fell from the bed and broke his neck.

None of us knows for certain how we will respond when facing off with Death for ourselves. If we cannot bring ourselves to being delighted to die, perhaps we can at least prepare our hearts to embrace death with dignity. My prayer is that this book will serve you well in providing a context of faith for your journey—now, and then.

My second motivation is to provide some assurance and encouragement for those who face a different kind of death, often daily—death to self. Paul put it this way:

---

[3] Ecclesiastes 3:2

I have been crucified with Christ; it is no longer I who live, but Christ lives in me; and the life which I now live in the flesh I live by faith in the Son of God, who loved me and gave Himself for me.[4]

There are so many sincere believers who would agree with Paul theoretically, but realistically do not own this testimony. Their lives speak primarily of self-preservation.

I do not question their sincerity. Neither do I question their plight. Many are spiritually paralyzed because of the actions, reactions, or inaction of those in their lives—past and/or present—who represent the authority of God. Rejection is very real! Abuse is very real! Yes, there are those who take unfair advantage of their positions at the expense of others.

I can only draw the conclusion that such victims have not been properly discipled and equipped for their roles in the priesthood ministry of Christ. Jesus does not leave us orphans; He comes to us and shows us how to respond to rejection, abuse, and abandonment—all the issues that are common to mankind.

Why make peace with the orphan spirit when you have been adopted as a son of God? Why live with the residual effects of any form of misuse or abuse when the gospel provision can make you an

[4] Galatians 2:20

overcomer? Why settle for being a victim when you are meant to be victorious?

Bottom line, it's up to you—your responsibility to embrace and obey the holistic gospel of Christ and His kingdom.

Introduction

More than thirty years ago, prior to my first trip to India, C. L. Moore[1] was praying for me. He prophesied:

"The time is short for India. There is coming a blood bath. The streets will flow with the blood of martyrs."

The atrocities in Orissa State and other places in India in recent years have fulfilled this prophecy in tragically literal ways. History is laced with similar seasons in other nations. We grieve at such reports, even as did our predecessors. We pray, even as did those who came before us. We try to understand, but cannot.

Recently, here in the United States of America, a denominational minister who is close to some of our family members attempted suicide. I don't know what he has been going through. But, I know what some of you are going through, and I cannot imagine how his situation could be more difficult than yours.

Why do some people kill? Why are others killed? Why do some despair to the point of taking their own lives? How should we live?

---

[1] C. L. Moore was at the time an elderly prophet from Oklahoma.

"When the Lord reveals His will to us and we obey, our mission will be a success regardless of the results."[2]

We found the believers with whom we met in China to be filled with the joy of the Lord, preoccupied with mission, and living with internal praise and worship as a lifestyle. All of them suffer persecution. All of them are subject to arrest and torture, even death, at any moment. Some of them had been imprisoned and beaten before we were there; others since we were there.

They live life moment-to-moment in the Spirit, and manifest the fruit of the Spirit. The church is strategically "underground," but growing daily through the bold, fearless and faithful witness of those who have settled The death issue, and found the joy of the Lord to be their strength.

"The call to Christ is a call to come and die."[3]

Please pray that our brethren in China, India, the African nations, the Middle East, and other places who are faced with persecution will be strengthened in faith and filled with the Holy Spirit. Pray that those who face death will look into open heavens and see Jesus, so that they may ask forgiveness for those who oppress them, as Stephen did.

---

[2] Chinese underground church leaders

[3] Dietrich Boenhoffer

Please also pray for believers in all countries to constantly be filled with and walk in the Spirit, that we may endure to the end ~ and be saved. We have the promise of eternal life in the kingdom of God, a promise worth dying for.

Who shall separate us from the love of Christ? Shall tribulation, or distress, or persecution, or famine, or nakedness, or peril, or sword? As it is written: "For Your sake we are killed all day long; we are accounted as sheep for the slaughter."

For I am persuaded that neither death nor life, nor angels nor principalities nor powers, nor things present nor things to come, nor height nor depth, nor any other created thing, shall be able to separate us from the love of God which is in Christ Jesus our Lord.[4]

Why did the Holy Spirit inspire Paul to write these words?

God, determining to show more abundantly to the heirs of promise the immutability of His counsel, confirmed it by an oath, that two immutable things, in which it is impossible for God to lie, we might have strong consolation, who have fled for refuge to lay hold of the hope set before us. This hope we have as an anchor of the soul, both sure and steadfast, and which enters the Presence behind the veil, where the forerunner has entered for us, even Jesus, having

[4] Romans 8:35-39

become High Priest forever according to the order of Melchizedek.[5]

For we know that the whole creation groans and labors with birth pangs together until now. Not only that, but we also who have the firstfruits of the Spirit, even we ourselves groan within ourselves, eagerly waiting for the adoption, the redemption of our body.

For we were saved in this hope, but hope that is seen is not hope; for why does one still hope for what he sees? But if we hope for what we do not see, we eagerly wait for it with perseverance.

"What if Christianity is not about enduring this sinful, fallen world in search of a reward of eternal rest? What if God brings together heaven and earth in a wholly new, wholly redeemed creation?"[6]

Hmmm.

---

[5] Hebrews 6:17-20

[6] From "Rethinking Heaven" by Jon Meacham, published in the April 16, 2012 edition of Time Magazine

Chapter 1

Losing Loved Ones

January 2004, we were called to our second daughter's home to hear unwelcome news. The testing had verified the worst in human terms—an inoperable malignant tumor was intertwined in her brain. It was an aggressive form of cancer. Two surgeries and numerous radiation and chemo treatments proved futile.

A loving family—doting husband, one son and three daughters, along with their respective spouses—parents, uncles, and aunts, surrounded Diane. The atmosphere was God-honoring worship. Praise music filled the home. Diane herself had chosen the course of believing for her healing. She was both valiant and resilient in hope. Just eight months passed between diagnosis and death.

She was forty-five and in the prime of life. Her mission had ended; her race was completed.

Shepherding a local congregation along with her husband, Diane was an inspiring worshipper and worship leader. She was a servant-leader throughout her life, a significant part of our family of ministers, and a holistic blessing to the communities where she lived as an adult. Who would have thought that her time to die would come before ours?

For eight months the shadow of death hovered over Diane, her family and friends. A haunting black cloud affected all who knew and loved her. There was no escape—no light in the tunnel. Yet, the nail-pierced hands held us close to Father's heart as we realized—perhaps more fully than ever before—just how fleeting life can be, and how dependent we are upon our God who is fully *love in action*.

There's an opportune time to do things, a right time for everything on the earth:

A right time for birth and another for death, a right time to plant and another to reap.

I've also concluded that whatever God does, that's the way it's going to be, always. No addition, no subtraction. God's done it and that's it. That's so we'll quit asking questions and simply worship in holy fear.

> *What was, is.*
> *Whatever will be, is.*
> *That's how it always is with God.*[1]

We should not mistake God's sovereignty for futility.

---

[1] Ecclesiastes 3:1-2, 14-15 TM

Paul's Perspective from a Better Covenant

Have you ever come on anything quite like this extravagant generosity of God, this deep, deep wisdom? It's way over our heads. We'll never figure it out.

Is there anyone around who can explain God? Anyone smart enough to tell Him what to do? Anyone who has done Him such a huge favor that God has to ask his advice?

> *Everything comes from Him;*
> *Everything happens through Him;*
> *Everything ends up in Him.*
> *Always glory! Always praise!*
> *Yes. Yes. Yes.*[2]

The Trust Factor

How unbelievers cope with the loss of a loved one is beyond my understanding. We who know, love, and trust our Father struggle with such crisis, even with His help. A firm grip on His hand enables us to *walk through the valley of the shadow of death* without fearing evil. The "trust factor" kicks into "automatic" without any capacity on our parts to understand or explain. You just don't know until you've been there, and done that.

---

[2] Romans 11:34-35 TM

We saw Doug and Linda, my brother and sister-in-law, grip His hand tightly as He helped them walk through that valley, coping with the added dimension of *shock*. They found their daughter's body. She was murdered, shot in the head at point-blank range. The father of her child will spend the rest of his life in prison, and the child is being raised by his grandparents—a constant reminder to them of the daughter they loved—and lost. Missy was thirty-six.

Thirty years earlier, Mark—a twenty-three-year-old disciple—had proposed to his sweetheart, Cher, on the night before going scuba diving in the Pacific Ocean. He never came back.

Why? He had so much potential. He and Cher were such a beautiful couple, sold-out followers of Jesus. Both guitarists and vocalists, they made beautiful music together. Our entire community shared in the shock and the grief.

Those were the days of singing Scripture songs. Mark and Cher especially liked to sing Psalm 139. Cher courageously sang it at Mark's memorial service:

> *"Where can I go from Your Spirit?*
> *Or where can I flee from Your presence?*
> *If I ascend into heaven, You are there;*
> *If I make my bed in hell, behold, You are there.*

"If I take the wings of the morning,
And dwell in the uttermost parts of the sea,
Even there Your hand shall lead me;
And Your right hand shall hold me."[3]

Oh, how God's presence filled that chapel as she sang. None of us would have been surprised to see Mark sit up and step out of that casket. But, God had another plan in mind. Several people committed their lives to Christ that day.

"Listen carefully: Unless a grain of wheat is buried in the ground, dead to the world, it is never any more than a grain of wheat. But if it is buried, it sprouts and reproduces itself many times over. In the same way, anyone who holds on to life just as it is destroys that life. But if you let it go, reckless in your love, you'll have it forever, real and eternal."[4]

Barbara Tells This Story

"One couple in the church gave birth to a baby girl who was born without a liver. Needless to say, this little baby became our top-priority prayer project. Her parents took her to various ministries, looking for her healing. They received many 'prophecies' that she was going to be healed.

---

[3] Psalm 139:7-10
[4] John 12:24-25 TM

"We all had opportunities to walk the floor with little Amy, and the entire church loved her as our own. We all 'stood in faith' for her healing, and were certain that God was going to let us keep her here on this earth. She was one-year-old when He chose to take her to be with Him. We were shocked and devastated at her death.

"'What about all of the prophecies that He would heal her?' Through this painful experience, we learned that people often "prophecy" from their own desires, thinking that this **must** be God's will.

God's Message came to me: "Son of man, preach against the prophets of Israel who are making things up out of their own heads and calling it 'prophesying.' Preach to them the real thing. Tell them, 'Listen to ***God's*** *Message!'"*[5]

"These are well-meaning saints, but they have not heard from God, and their good intentions can cause much confusion and hurt.

"For a long time I kept asking my Lord, 'Why did You take Amy when we were trusting You to heal her?' He was silent.

Then, one day, several months later, I was reading the Word,

---

[5] Ezekiel 13:1-2 TM

For I am persuaded that neither death nor life, nor angels nor principalities nor powers, nor things present nor things to come, nor height nor depth, nor any other created thing, shall be able to separate us from the love of God which is in Christ Jesus our Lord.[6]

"The word **death** seemed to jump off of the page! As long as I was questioning my Lord, I was doubting His wisdom. And I had allowed Amy's death to separate me from His love to the extent that I was doubting!

"I quickly repented, and prayed, 'Father, I don't **ever** have to understand why! You are Lord! I do trust You.' Instantly, my soul was at peace for the first time since her death.

"Isn't going to be with Him the perfect healing?"

We Are Not Without Hope

I do not want you to be ignorant, brethren, concerning those who have fallen asleep, lest you sorrow as others who have no hope. For if we believe that Jesus died and rose again, even so God will bring with Him those who sleep in Jesus.[7]

I remember my last visit to my faithful translator in India. Several years my senior, Lt. Col. Joseph Daniel,

---

[6] Romans 8:37-39

[7] 1 Thessalonians 4:13-14

retired from a lifetime of service in the Salvation Army, was living out his last days in the home of his daughter. He was watching for me from the porch as I made my way up the path. Past ninety, he began to jump up and down, and clap his hands, the moment he saw me. We clung to one another, and wept. We had enjoyed many years of devoted friendship, serving God together with one another.

We had moved in the Spirit as one man—I speaking, him translating—same inflections, the same movements, even the same body language. If I crowed like a chicken, Joseph Daniel crowed like a chicken. If I barked like a dog, he barked like a dog. This was a partnership authored in heaven, for sure.

We heard of his death just a few weeks later. I grieved. I celebrated.

And then there was the man who had obviously been sleeping in a boxcar on the railroad siding. He apparently got up in the night, fell down the bank, and did not have the strength to climb back to his shelter from the cold. I was hunting with my uncle. His body was in my pathway. The State buried him without friend, relative, or even a name.

Jesus was only thirty-three.

Chapter 2

Acquainted With Grief

There are probably no two people whose experiences with grief follow exactly the same pattern. Like fingerprints, they are uniquely our own. Our social and cultural experiences lend to us broadly varying emotional make-ups that manifest grief in ways that others may not understand. But, we can care.

Most of us have been found wanting in what to say to someone who has just lost a spouse, or a child, or a parent. Not many are proficient in coming up with the right words at times like this. Perhaps a warm embrace accompanied by a genuine smile—with love coming through our eyes from the depths of our soul is enough for that moment.

Jesus was *acquainted with grief* in its broadest sense and application. He is the one Person in our lives who knows exactly what to do and what to say at every moment, and in every circumstance. He is the Father who cares and the Spirit who comforts. Isaiah prophesied:

He is despised and rejected by men, a Man of sorrows and acquainted with grief.[1]

---

[1] Isaiah 53:3a

Jesus told His disciples, *"You shall be hated by all men for My name's sake."*[2] His life in us can reveal to us how to handle being *despised and rejected.* He knows all about *sorrows and grief*—been there. Done that!

It should not be too much of a stretch for us to grasp that—within the context of our oneness with Him—He is the One who completely understands, who *can be touched with the feeling of our infirmities.*[3]

Many Believers Live in Denial about Death

"I see this whole death denial thing as a major issue in our culture and in the body of Christ. There is such an illusion that only wonderful things are supposed to happen to us. When death happens, it comes as a "shock," an interruption to this wonderful life we have planned for ourselves. Many suddenly find themselves with an inability to cope with what we call "grief." When death, the uninvited and unannounced visitor comes, it often results in emotional and life disintegration for so many."[4]

Death is an inevitable and undeniable reality. It is a part of life. The first step to preparing is to stop denying, and ask God to build His inner strength into our characters so that we can face tomorrow.

---

[2] Luke 21:17
[3] Hebrews 4:15 KJV
[4] Dr. Stephen Crosby

Barbara and I have been married for fifty-eight years. Neither of us can imagine life without the other.

There are a few options:

- We could harden our hearts toward one another; purposely move away from one another, so that we might minimize the grief and pain that comes with the loss of a loved one.

- We could live in denial and conduct our life together as though it will never end.

- Or, we could simply realize that there will be an interruption in the midst of our passionate love for one another. A sudden ending to a lifetime of unmitigated joy together will transition us into the next phase that our God has for us.

  "Should you go first and I remain
  to finish with the scroll,
  No less than shadows shall ever creep in
  to make this life seem droll.
  We've known so much of happiness
  we've had our cup of joy,
  And memory is one gift of God
  that death cannot destroy."[5]

[5] From "Beyond the Sunset" by Virgil and Blanche Brock

Jesus wept. I weep a lot! Nostalgia, patriotism, shared emotions, and those unusual times of spiritual insights or breakthroughs, can trigger tears from these old eyes. It doesn't take much to touch my heart. I believe that I have been granted the honor of feeling a tad of what Father feels.

It is a special privilege to be able to feel deeply for others, known or unknown, next door or on the other side of the globe.

Grief is more than deep feelings and tears. Searing and seemingly endless pain of the soul makes grief seem unbearable at times. It is not to be "stuffed." But, it must not rule. It is to be ruled.

For the believer, grief is to be governed by the Holy Spirit.

Horatio G. Spafford's only son was killed by scarlet fever at the age of four. A year later, it was fire rather than fever that struck. Horatio had invested heavily in real estate on the shores of Lake Michigan. In 1871, every one of these holdings was wiped out by the great Chicago Fire.

Aware of the toll that these disasters had taken on the family, Horatio decided to take his wife and four daughters on a holiday to England. And so, the Spaffords traveled to New York in November, from where they were to catch the French steamer 'Ville de

Havre' across the Atlantic. Yet just before they set sail, a last-minute business development forced Horatio to delay. Not wanting to ruin the family holiday, Spafford persuaded his family to go as planned. He would follow on later. With this decided, Anna and her four daughters sailed East to Europe while Spafford returned West to Chicago. Just nine days later, Spafford received a telegram from his wife in Wales. It read: "Saved alone."

On November 2, 1873, the 'Ville de Havre' had collided with 'The Lochearn', an English vessel. It sank in only 12 minutes, claiming the lives of 226 people. Anna Spafford had stood bravely on the deck, with her daughters Annie, Maggie, Bessie and Tanetta clinging desperately to her. Her last memory had been of her baby being torn violently from her arms by the force of the waters. Anna was only saved from the fate of her daughters by a plank which floated beneath her unconscious body and propped her up. When the survivors of the wreck had been rescued, Mrs. Spafford's first reaction was one of complete despair. Then she heard a voice speak to her, "You were spared for a purpose." And she immediately recalled the words of a friend, "It's easy to be grateful and good when you have so much, but take care that you are not a fair-weather friend to God."

Upon hearing the terrible news, Horatio Spafford boarded the next ship out of New York to join his bereaved wife. Bertha Spafford (the fifth daughter of

Horatio and Anna born later) explained that during her father's voyage, the captain of the ship had called him to the bridge. "A careful reckoning has been made", he said, "and I believe we are now passing the place where the de Havre was wrecked. The water is three miles deep." Horatio then returned to his cabin and penned the lyrics of his great hymn.

> "When peace like a river, attendeth my way,
> When sorrows like sea billows roll;
> Whatever my lot, Thou hast taught me to say,
> 'It is well, it is well with my soul.'"

Chapter 3

Loving Life

"Wrong attitudes will block the blessings of God and cause us to live below God's purpose for our lives."[1]

The loss of loved ones is part of living. Grief points us to the Comforter—not necessarily for understanding, but for consolation and comfort. His presence and power will soon yield confidence in our destiny and strength for the journey.

Until we are eyeball-to-eyeball, trying to stare down Death ourselves, we cannot—and should not—question others' experiences, decisions and directions. God intends for us to love life—thrusting ourselves into every opportunity to experience His creation.

> *God, my shepherd!*
> *I don't need a thing.*
> *You have bedded me down in lush meadows,*
> *You find me quiet pools to drink from.*
> *True to Your word, You let me catch my breath*
> *and send me in the right direction.*[2]

---

[1] John Maxwell
[2] Psalm 23:1-3 TM

God in Nature, in People

We took our lunch to a park today. Walking toward an unoccupied picnic table, we passed by a huge multi-level bird feeder designed to accommodate many varieties of our winged friends at the same time. More than a dozen squirrels were scurrying around the base of the feeder, enjoying the seeds that fell to the ground.

Neither of us could decide whether that lone swimmer was a long-necked duck or a short-necked goose. It had the colorful markings of a male Mallard. But, that neck? Just about that time we were distracted by a jumping fish, and avoided making a decision—duck or goose?

Some distance away, children were playing on the playground under the watchful eyes of their mothers. A grandfather was getting exercise by picking up pine cones, putting them into his grandson's plastic bucket, so that he might throw them to the ground again. Life is not always equitable. But, it is to be celebrated. Life is a good thing!

Jesus Tied His Coming to Our Lives

"I have come that they may have life, and have it more abundantly."[3]

---

[3] John 10:10

This *abundant life* does not wait for the afterlife. We are the benefactors of the resurrection life of Christ right here, and right now. Where do we go to find it? A telling question.

The earlier revelation (the old covenant) *was intended simply to get us ready for the Messiah, Who then puts everything right for those who trust Him to do it. Moses wrote that anyone who insists on using the law code to live right before God soon discovers it's not so easy— every detail of life regulated by fine print! But trusting God to shape the right living in us is a different story—no precarious climb up to heaven to recruit the Messiah, no dangerous descent into hell to rescue the Messiah. So what exactly was Moses saying?*

The word that saves is right here,
as near as the tongue in your mouth,
as close as the heart in your chest.

It's the word of faith that welcomes God to go to work and set things right for us.[4]

"When Jesus was raised He became the ultimate pattern of manhood for the world. Jesus fulfilled the vision in Father's heart of what mankind—sons—were meant to be, the plumbline of God's righteousness."[5]

---

[4] Romans 10:4-10 TM
[5] Brian Harrison

This is what happened in baptism. When we went under the water, we left the old country of sin behind; when we came up out of the water, we entered into the new country of grace—a new life.

That's what baptism into the life of Jesus means.[6]

The abundance of the Christ life within us provides the necessary stamina to live this life "pedal to the metal," accelerating through many trials, tribulations, and persecutions. When we value life with this eternal measuring rod, everything we experience becomes worthwhile—even the loss of loved ones.

"My grace is enough, it's all you need. My strength comes into its own in your weakness."[7]

"May the blessing of light be upon you, light on the outside and light on the inside. With God's sunlight shining on you, may your heart glow with warmth like a turf fire that welcomes friends and strangers alike.

"May the light of the Lord shine from your eyes like a candle in the window, welcoming the weary traveler.

"May the blessing of God's soft rain be on you, falling gently on your head, refreshing your soul with the sweetness of little flowers newly blooming.

---

[6] Romans 6:2-3 TM
[7] 2 Corinthians 12:9 TM

"May the strength of the winds of Heaven bless you, carrying the rain to wash your spirit clean, sparkling after, in the sunlight.

"May the blessing of God's earth be on you and as you walk the roads, may you always have a kind word for those you meet.

"May you understand the strength and power of God in a thunderstorm in winter, the quiet beauty of creation and the calm of a summer sunset.

"And may you come to realize that insignificant as you may seem in this great universe, you are an important part of God's plan.

"May He watch over you and keep you safe from harm. "[8]

---

[8] Irish Blessing – Lyrics by Phil Coulter

Chapter 4

Fighting to Live

Tony Greene was born in Boone, North Carolina, October 17, 1968. In addition to being noted as a gifted lead vocalist, Tony has also been included in the list of leading concert promoters of Southern Gospel music.

Tony married TaRanda February 13, 2001. They served the Lord and the Lord's people in gospel music, and eventually had two children.

On August 25, 2009, Tony underwent a successful kidney transplant. His wife, TaRanda, was the donor. We were present the Sunday before, when Tony and TaRanda came for prayer.

He returned to traveling within a month and though he encountered some minor health difficulties, he continued with the Greenes until additional health issues forced his hospitalization on September 21, 2010.

One week later, on September 28, Tony passed from this life just a few weeks before his forty-second birthday.

These two did everything they could to keep Tony alive. TaRanda[1] put her own life on the line. Thousands prayed. Tony died.

Go figure.

Jose and Monica Bosque's little granddaughter died after fighting a rare form of leukemia for six months. The family was devastated. It is easy to understand why people question God. Only His grace can keep us from bitterness and its destructive influence in our lives.

A Personal Testimony

Nearly twenty years ago, Barbara and I were living in Pennsylvania. On one particular weekend, we were about four hours away from our home, visiting and ministering in a local fellowship.

Saturday night came, and I spoke to a group of young adults. Feeling feverish, I didn't stay for refreshments, but went to bed. I was up several times during the night, in the bathroom, without much result.

---

[1] After 13 years of ministry with one of Southern Gospel music's most beloved family trios, The Greenes, TaRanda Greene has decided to continue her calling and ministry as a soloist.

God's grace got me through the Sunday morning meeting, and we headed home, stopping at every turnpike rest area. I would run into the men's room, to no avail.

I was in the emergency room at 6 a.m. Monday, having my first experience with a catheter. As unpleasant as I had always feared, the immediate relief made the procedure worthwhile to say the least.

I saw an urologist on Tuesday morning. He removed the catheter, did a sonogram, and did a biopsy of my prostate.

I was back in his office on Wednesday morning because I desperately needed to be catheterized again.

Friday I was on a plane to St. Louis, where I was scheduled to speak at a men's conference. I called Barbara just before the opening session. She shared with me the pathologist report on the biopsy.

The urologist confirmed the presence of cancer, and briefly told her that if the cancer had gotten beyond the prostate, I was not going to live. (Nice guy, but totally untrained in how to break this kind of news to someone's wife!)

I tried to comfort my wife as best as I could, long distance by phone.

By this time I was being introduced. I immediately greeted everyone, "Cathy and I are delighted to be here with you today!"

Well, you can imagine the confusion on the faces—especially those who know Barbara! I immediately went on to explain that "Cathy" was my catheter, and shared the doctor's prognosis. Then I said, "The doctor says that I have cancer in my body, and the Word and Spirit say that I have Jesus in my body! Greater is He who is in me, than cancer! We are here to kick devil-butt this weekend."

Resignation and Redirection

I decided on the flight home that, if this was "it" for me in this life, we needed to quickly move back to North Carolina where we would be surrounded with children and grandchildren.[2] We were on the road home within days.

A local urologist explained that, with this kind of cancer, there is not a need to panic or head to the operating table immediately. He prescribed a strong antibiotic to fight the prostatitis.

---

[2] It is not *unbelief* to wisely prepare for death so that loved ones are not left in the dark concerning business, personal, and family matters. Jesus prepared John as he laid his head on His breast. He imparted the love of a son that would be adequate for John's caring of Jesus' mother.

My posture was total surrender to the Lord's will. Nothing in me was willing to fight. But, Barbara asked the Father about His will, could not get peace, and so she fought. And, I was healed.

Go figure.

The Gospel, A Matter of Life and Death

So many understand the gospel to be about being *right* or *wrong*, or being *good* or *evil*. Those issues can be resolved at *the tree of the knowledge of good and evil.* But, that is forbidden fruit, forbidden territory.[3]

All have sinned and fall short of the glory of God.[4]

The wages of sin is death, but the gift of God is eternal life in Christ Jesus our Lord.[5]

"For God so loved the world that He gave His only begotten Son, that whoever believes in Him should not perish, but have everlasting life"'[6]

So we see that the gospel is about being dead or alive! For the believer, it's some of both: We are *dead to sin, but alive to God in Christ Jesus!*[7]

---

[3] Genesis 2:15-17
[4] Romans 3:23
[5] Romans 6:23
[6] John 3:16
[7] Romans 6:11

All have sinned. The wages of sin is death. Therefore, our spirit man is dead, no matter how good we grow up to be.

But, *the gift of God is eternal life in Christ Jesus our Lord.* Therefore, all who believe in, rely upon, and trust in Jesus are made eternally alive, no matter how bad and evil we grew up to be.

The good news is about Jesus, and His love for and availability to us. His reward for those who are His: everlasting life. Identifying the exact moment of divine transaction—giving up the old life that has been operating out of death, and taking up the new life that operates out of life—but, who cares?

"Be guided, only by the healer of the sick, the raiser of the dead, the friend of all who were afflicted and forlorn, the patient Master who shed tears of compassion for our infirmities. We cannot but be right when we put all the rest away, and do everything in remembrance of Him...There can be no confusion in following Him, and seeking for no other footsteps, I am certain!"[8]

---

[8] Charles Dickens

Chapter 5

"Choosing Life"

"Choose for yourselves this day whom you will serve, whether the gods which your fathers served that were on the other side of the River, or the gods of the Amorites, in whose land you dwell. But as for me and my house, we will serve the Lord."

So the people answered and said: "Far be it from us that we should forsake the Lord to serve other gods; for the Lord our God is He who brought us and our fathers up out of the land of Egypt, from ***the house of bondage****, who did those great signs in our sight, and* ***preserved us in all the way that we went and among all the people through whom we passed."***[1]

From the moment of my decision and surrender to the Lord Jesus to this day—nearly fifty years—the Lord our God has:

- Kept me from the house of bondage, and
- Preserved me in all the way I went and
- Among all the people through whom I passed

The house of bondage has many rooms. They are the counterparts of Father's house that has many mansions. Bondage is bondage, no matter how you

[1] Joshua 24:15-17

dice it or dress it. We cannot pass the buck. The root of all bondage is the life of Adam in which we all have our start. The corporate image is *narcissism;* the corporate platform is *entitlements.* It's all about me. It's all about us.

It is this Adam life that must go, so that the Christ life may emerge! Adam's fear of death[2] motivates the raging battle to keep people in bondage. Jesus has kept me from *the house of bondage.*

He also *preserved me in all the way I went.* Adam would have been so vulnerable to contagious sickness and disease. I remember visiting a friend in the hospital. His roommate was delirious. I laid hands on him and prayed for him. He settled into a peaceful sleep. The hospital called the next day after finding that the man had a highly contagious disease, and urged me to come for inoculation. I assured them that there was no need for that. For, *greater is He who is in me than he who is in the world.*[3]

Flying and driving millions of miles accident-free in itself defied the odds and scrambled the averages. The rules of the game are canceled for those who are in Christ.

You've got to know that among *all of the people through whom I passed,* there had to be some very nasty and

---

[2] Hebrews 2:15

[3] 1 John 4:4

irreverent confrontations. Had Adam been allowed to live in me, I would have been rejected, wounded, and marginalized. But, praise God, the new creation cannot be touched, even by the most violent ways of man or beast.

Whatever I have been through, whomever I have encountered, our Father has shown me how to become *better* rather than *bitter.* Understanding that His Spirit does lead us *into the wilderness,*[4] invites Satan to *consider* us,[5] and causes *everything to work together for our good,*[6] we find ourselves without excuse. We can cast *all of our cares upon Him, for He cares for* us.[7]

Forgiveness

Jesus prayed from the cross for the forgiveness of those who nailed Him there.[8] Stephen, employing his last few breaths, prayed for Father to forgive those who were stoning him to death in their ignorance.[9] Paul and Silas sang praises to Him at midnight while shackled in the inner prison.[10]

---

[4] Luke 4:1
[5] Job 1:8
[6] Romans 8:28
[7] 1 Peter 5:7
[8] Luke 23:34; also see Isaiah 53:12
[9] Acts 7:60
[10] Acts 16:25

After receiving a model prayer for His disciples, Jesus explained,

"For if you forgive men their trespasses, your heavenly Father will also forgive you. But if you do not forgive men their trespasses, neither will your Father forgive your trespasses."[11]

I am so thankful for the foundations learned early on that equipped me to *return good for evil, turn the other cheek, go another mile, and give away my shirt.* I have been blessed to recognize that my *warfare is not with flesh and blood.*[12] Therefore, I can *love my enemies and pray for those who persecute me.*[13]

There have been times when He provided a teacher to model, show, and instruct me regarding how to act or respond. There have also been times when the Teacher did that by Himself. Bottom line, *the anointing teaches* us,[14] and we are without excuse.

No experience, whether by devils or men, has been able to distract or damage me. My choices are mine to own. I am responsible for my own destiny. I have given Him my heart. And, He is keeping and preserving me.

---

[11] Matthew 6:14-15
[12] Ephesians 6:12
[13] Sermon on the Mount
[14] 1 John 2:27

For I am persuaded that neither death nor life, nor angels nor principalities nor powers, nor things present nor things to come, nor height nor depth, nor any other created thing, shall be able to separate us from the love of God which is in Christ Jesus our Lord.[15]

Making Choices is a Heart Matter

We must choose to be offended, to cling to unforgiveness, to be wounded. We must realize that the new creation man, who we really are, cannot be offended. Only that old man who was to have been crucified with Christ can cling to such issues. *For you have died, and your life is hidden with Christ in God.*[16] The life that is set before us to live is His life.

Every offense presents us with an opportunity to crucify the flesh and forgive from the heart, in the Spirit of the Redeemer. That's what mature believers do!

Mature believers who are sons led by the Spirit do not sit around licking the wounds of a dead man!

"See, I have set before you today life and good, death and evil, in that I command you today to love the Lord your God, to walk in His ways, and to keep His commandments, His statutes, and His judgments, that you may live and

---

[15] Romans 8:38-39

[16] Colossians 3:3

multiply; and the Lord your God will bless you in the land which you go to possess.

*"But **if your heart turns away so that you do not hear**, and are drawn away, and worship other gods and serve them, I announce to you today that you shall surely perish; you shall not prolong your days in the land which you cross over the Jordan to go in and possess.*

*"I call heaven and earth as witnesses today against you, that I have set before you life and death, blessing and cursing; therefore **choose life**, that both you and your descendants may live; that you may love the Lord your God, that you may obey His voice, and that you may cling to Him, for He is your life and the length of your days; and that you may dwell in the land which the Lord swore to your fathers, to Abraham, Isaac, and Jacob, to give them."*[17]

No one can make our choices for us. For, even if pressures from another push us to make wrong decisions, we are still responsible for those decisions. The "blame game" will be useless in the Day of Judgment.

Those who take up offenses for the abused rather than leading them to the Cross empower them in their Adam lives.

---

[17] Deuteronomy 30:15-20

- Either we are *born again*, or we are not.[18]
- Either we are *a new creation*, or we are not.[19]
- Either we have the life of Jesus Christ within us, or we do not.[20]
- Either Jesus is Lord, or He is not.[21]

There are no legitimate third parties involved at the bottom line. God cannot be blamed for our decisions, for the choices we make.

If you confess with your mouth the Lord Jesus and ***believe in your heart*** *that God raised Him from the dead, you will be saved. For* ***with the heart one believes unto righteousness****, and with the mouth confession is made unto salvation.*[22]

The God of Peace Guards Our Hearts and Minds

Rejoice in the Lord always. Again I will say, rejoice! Let your gentleness be known to all men. The Lord is at hand.

Be anxious for nothing, but in everything by prayer and supplication, with thanksgiving, let your requests be made known to God; and the peace of God, which surpasses all

---

[18] John 3:3-8
[19] 2 Corinthians 5:17
[20] 2 Corinthians 13:5; Colossians 1:27
[21] Matthew 7:21-27; Luke 6:46-49
[22] Romans 10:9-10

understanding, will guard your hearts and minds through Christ Jesus.[23]

I know whom I have believed and am persuaded that He is able to keep what I have committed to Him until that Day.[24]

"You will have no test of faith that will not fit you to be a blessing if you are obedient to the Lord. I never had a trial but when I got out of the deep river I found some poor pilgrim on the bank that I was able to help by that very experience."[25]

---

[23] Philippians 4:4-7
[24] 2 Timothy 1:12
[25] A. B. Simpson

Chapter 6

Avoiding Death Traps

There has been at least one play, one film, a book, three songs, a hypothetical organism, and a video game, about *Deathtrap*. There is also a motorcycle club bearing that name.

You may wonder how such a chapter title could find its way into a book that pertains to the life and kingdom of God. Good question!

Jesus warned:

"If anyone tries to flag you down, calling out, 'Here's the Messiah!' or points, 'There He is!' don't fall for it. Fake Messiah's and lying preachers are going to put up everywhere. Their impressive credentials and dazzling performances will pull the wool over the eyes of even those who ought to know better. But I've given you fair warning.

"So if they say, 'Run to the country and see Him arrive!' or 'Quick, get downtown, see Him come!' don't give them the time of day. The arrival of the Son of Man isn't something you go to see. He comes like swift lightning to you! "Whenever you see crowds gathering, think of carrion vultures circling, moving in, hovering over a rotting

carcass. You can be quite sure that it's not the living Son of Man pulling in those crowds."[1]

Allowing for the possibility that this particular prophecy was fulfilled in A.D. 70, the nature of people has not changed. The warning is pertinent to our day. It is absolutely amazing how naïve we believers can be.

Who can forget the Lakeland, Florida, debacle—with all of its "apostolic and prophetic proclamations, affirmations, and confirmations?"[2] While some flocked to Florida, others were making their way to a certain latitude and longitude in a barren place in Idaho. Because someone told them that there was a "portal" at that spot.

Religious Appetites vs. Spiritual Realities

The appetites for miracles, portals, things that sound mystical and appeal to the religious flesh are evidences of this naivety and lack of discernment.

A Bible search turned up absolutely nothing—not one reference to the word, portal, in Strong's Exhaustive Concordance of the Bible.

A Google search of the web for the meaning of "portal" resulted in the first two pages being given to

---

[1] Matthew 24:23-28 TM
[2] Show Biz at its worst, starring Todd Bentley

an action/puzzle video game. And then there was this definition:

"A **portal** in science fiction and fantasy is a magical or technological doorway that connects two distant locations separated by spacetime. It usually consists of two or more gateways, with an object entering one gateway leaving via the other instantaneously."

Persistence finally resulted in this definition: "A gate, door, or the extremeties (ends) of a tunnel."[3]

I would suggest that Jesus is our gate, our door, and the extremities (ends) of a tunnel. He is on the Throne in heaven, and also on the Throne in my innermost being. He said:

- *"I am the way, the truth and the life. No one comes to the Father except through Me."*[4]
- *"I am the door."*[5]
- *"Enter by the narrow gate that leads to life."*[6]

Jesus is Jacob's ladder—connecting heaven and earth. The Hebrew writer summarized our preferred position in Jesus in this way:

Let us therefore come boldly to the throne of grace, that we may obtain mercy and find grace to help in time of need.[7]

---

[3] Wikipedia
[4] John 14:6
[5] John 10:9
[6] Matthew 7:13

Another spiritual sounding term that makes us special is: "Something has shifted in the heavenlies!" No, something needs to be shifting on the earth, beginning within the hearts and minds of believers.

All of these religious expressions have the potential to be at least distractions, and possibly "death traps" to beguile and *deceive even the elect--if that were possible.*[8]

Lifelong trysts with familiar spirits are embraced, nurtured, and sustained by some who have a great need to believe that they are somehow special—more spiritual—than others.

Amos prophesied:

"I'll send a famine through the whole country. It won't be food or water that is lacking, but My Word. People will drift from one end of the country to the other, roam to the north, wander to the east. They'll go anywhere, listen to anyone, hoping to hear God's Word—but they won't hear it."[9]

The word that saves is right here, as near as the tongue in your mouth, as close as the heart in your chest.[10]

---

[7] Hebrews 4:16
[8] Matthew 24:24
[9] Amos 8:11-12 TM
[10] Romans 10:8 TM

O. C. Visitation vs. N. C. Habitation

Here's good news: This religious geek's name is *Adam*, and he is dead! He was *buried with Christ in baptism, that you (a new creation) might be raised to walk in newness of life.*[11]

No more need for wild goose chases or costly religious extravaganzas. All we need to do is live in Him and yield to Him as He lives in us.

We are, so to speak, God's portals. People can meet Him in us. We can be Jacob's ladder. We can stand between heaven and earth in intercession.

Our search for God has ended. He found us! He has come to abide in us. It's no longer about *visitation.* We are His *habitation.* It's not about latitude and longitude--has nothing to do with geography. As the psalmist asked,

> *Where can I go from Your Spirit?*
>
> *Where can I flee from Your presence?*[12]

Beware of religious death traps that appeal to our senses—especially our pride—that complicate and distract us from the simplicity that is in Christ.

---

[11] Romans 6:4
[12] Psalm 139:7

Chapter 7

Want to Be Somebody?

"God sends no-one away empty, except those who are full of themselves."[1]

Cult leaders are often egocentric power mongers with a great need to control people. Many or most of them may have started out in a legitimate Christian context, but were beguiled by false religious spirits when they were confronted with a choice between using demonically augmented soul power instead of remembering that we died with Jesus and now live in Him.

Leadership, a valid motivational gift,[2] can be used for personal gain or unselfish serving. The naivety of the normal new believer makes him especially vulnerable for nurture or exploitation. Paul revealed a fatherly heart in his communications with spiritually infant believers.

"Paul's first letter to the Corinthians is a classic of pastoral response: affectionate, firm, clear, and unswerving in the conviction that God among them, revealed in Jesus and present in His Holy Spirit,

---

[1] Dwight L. Moody

[2] Romans 12:8 – "He who leads, with diligence"

continued to be the central issue in their lives, regardless of how much of a mess they had made of things. Paul doesn't disown them as brother and sister Christians, doesn't throw them out because of their bad behavior, and doesn't fly into a tirade over their irresponsible ways. He takes it all more or less in stride, but also takes them by the hand and goes over all the old ground again, directing them in how to work all the glorious details of God's saving love into their love for one another."[3]

Paul began early in his epistle to remind them of what they did not bring with them into the faith:

Take a good look, friends, at who you were when you got called into this life. I don't see many of "the brightest and the best" among you, not many influential, not many from high society families. Isn't it obvious that God deliberately chose men and women that the culture overlooks and exploits and abuses, chose these "nobodies" to expose the hollow pretensions of the "somebodies"? That makes it quite clear that none of you can get by with blowing your own horn before God. Everything that we have—right thinking and right living, a clean slate and a fresh start—comes from God by way of Jesus Christ. That's why we have the saying, "If you're going to blow a horn, blow a trumpet for God.[4]

---

[3] From Eugene H. Peterson's Introduction to 1 Corinthians, The Message

[4] 1 Corinthians 1:26-31 TM

It took me a long time to finally come to grips with the futility of trying to be somebody or to do something for God!

So long as I tried to be somebody I remained a nobody. Only after I became willing to be nobody did Jesus begin to make me somebody.

The Death that Leads to Life

"Before He furnishes the abundant supply, we must first be made conscious of our emptiness. Before He gives strength, we must be made to feel our weakness. Slow, painfully slow, are we to learn this lesson; and slower still to own our nothingness and take the place of helplessness before the Mighty One."[5]

I have no valid identity apart from Him. Paul stated this in numerous ways:

- *I have been crucified with Christ; it is no longer I who live, but Christ lives in me; and the life which I now live in the flesh I live by faith in the Son of God, who loved me and gave Himself for me.*[6]

- *By the grace of God I am what I am, and His grace toward me was not in vain; but I labored more*

---

[5] A. W. Pink
[6] Galatians 2:20

abundantly than they all, yet not I but the grace of God which was with me.[7]

- *We have this treasure in earthen vessels, that the excellence of the power may be of God and not of us.*[8]

- *For we who live are always delivered to death for Jesus' sake, that the life of Jesus also may be manifested in our mortal flesh. So then death is working in us, but life in you.*[9]

The ultimate in fatherly affirmation was spoken by God when He declared Jesus' identity:

"This is My beloved Son, in whom I am well pleased. Hear Him."[10]

Being one among the many brothers whom God is bringing to glory, that's the only identity I desire.

I'm all eyes and ears![11]

---

[7] 1 Corinthians 15:10
[8] 2 Corinthians 4:7
[9] 2 Corinthians 4:11-12
[10] Matthew 17:5
[11] Matthew 13:16

Chapter 8

Unresolved Anger

I had taken a team to India. They were sitting behind me along with the pastor of the local church, as I was ministering to several dozen men and women who were sitting on the floor in front of me.

Acting on a word of knowledge, I invited a young man to the front. I was aware of a stirring in the crowd as I did so, and also could hear the pastor trying desperately to communicate something to the team members.

I prophesied to the young man that his heart was full of anger, but that Jesus was taking the anger from his heart, and he was going home that night without anger, a man of peace He fell to the floor under the power of the Spirit, and remained "as dead" for several minutes.

Following the dismissal, my teammates were eager to tell me that the pastor just kept saying, "Murder! Murder!" Upon investigating, we found that, indeed, the young man had been accused of murder. (We did not find out the legal status, or why he was free to attend this gathering.)

I inquired of God, and was shown that "anger" is a root of murder, and I had ministered according to the root rather than the fruit.

"You're familiar with the command to the ancients, 'Do not murder.' I'm telling you that anyone who is so much as angry with a brother or sister is guilty of murder."[1]

Believers are so often troubled by the actions of others, making their judgments on the basis of fruit rather than discerning the root. Since we are endowed with the life of Christ within, and empowered by His Spirit, we should wait for discernment and direction before lopping off what is above the surface. Weeds that are not pulled out by the root quickly grow back.

Judge a brother based merely on what you can see with the natural eye, and your reaction could damage that brother. When the Spirit grants you discernment, with wisdom, you are then able to be redemptive in your ministry to another.

Anger Needs Resolved, Not Merely Managed

Christ in you, through your being crucified with Him, lives and loves through you. His Spirit gives you gifts for the common good,[2] including *the discerning of*

---

[1] Matthew 5:21 TM
[2] 1 Corinthians 12:7

spirits. Then, the next step may be asking Him to give you a *word of wisdom,* that will facilitate redemptive directions for fruitful interaction.

Your crucifixion/death[3] facilitates the releasing of Jesus' resurrection life from within you. You thereby become incarnational and missional, and it is no longer simply one person trying to correct another person.

The sweet aroma of heaven will attend your words, and the anointing will break yokes off of others.

There are no shortcuts. Heaven's life does not initiate from *this body of death.*[4] Life emanates from the hearts of believers like a river.

"If anyone thirsts, let him come to Me and drink. He who believes in Me, as the Scripture has said, out of his heart will flow rivers of living water." But this He spoke concerning the Spirit whom those believing in Him would receive.[5]

Because of the indwelling Spirit, we are able to be angry, and sin not. The moment that we experience anger rising up in us, we can surrender it to the Holy Spirit within, and receive heaven's counsel regarding His sanctified anger management.

---

[3] Romans 6:4; Galatians 2:20

[4] Romans 7:24

[5] John 7:37b-39a

Therefore, putting away lying, "Let each one of you speak truth with his neighbor," for we are members of one another.

"Be angry, and do not sin." Do not let the sun go down on your wrath, nor give place to the devil.[6]

"The woman wanted on assault charges is in custody Monday morning after officials say she poured a pot of hot grease on a crowd of people Sunday."[7]

Six, including a one-year-old and three other children, were rushed to the Burn Center in Winston-Salem with severe burns. Cause? Anger between neighbors!

Should one or more of these victims die, what began as anger will have escalated to murder.

Regardless of issue or motive, it would have been better for one or both of these people to die to self, to ego, to pride, to fear, to insecurity, etc., and let Jesus flow like a river into that situation, enabling someone to return good for evil, even overcoming evil with good.

Someone who had been crucified with Christ, buried with Him in the waters of baptism, raised to walk in newness of life, and to invade and engage the desperate world we live in with love that never fails.

---

[6] Ephesians 4:25-27

[7] News report from Charlotte, NC, Father's Day 2012

The news reports did not indicate that there were any men present—only women and children. Unfortunately, this is just another report of domestic violence—daily routine, in our fatherless society and orphan culture. Charlotte Police answer an average of ninety-eight domestic violence reports every day—nearly thirty-six thousand each year.

So, we may conclude that murder is often the fruit of unresolved anger. But,

A Common Root of Anger

Fathers, do not provoke your children to wrath, but bring them up in the training and admonition of the Lord.[8]

It is beyond the scope of this book to detail this topic.[9] Briefly, all that a father needs to do to provoke children to anger is NOTHING! Fatherless children grow up angry and unprepared for life, because it is the fathers' privilege and duty under God to *bring them up in the training and admonition of God.*

The first place for the practice of self-denial—death to self—is in the home where wives are to be loved and children are to be nurtured and trained.

---

[8] Ephesians 6:4

[9] This topic is dealt with in more detail in my book, "Like Father, Like Son" available at DonAtkin.com.

Chapter 9

No Retaliation

You may be ticked to the max! But, to follow your carnal instincts would be a denial of your true position in Christ. God's capacity with you empowers you to suck it up, and forgive.

No, I'm not saying that the offender will get off free. But, the rules of engagement are radically different in the kingdom of heaven. They usually offend the old nature—aha—providing another opportunity to *reckon yourselves dead indeed to sin, but alive to God in Christ Jesus or Lord.*[1]

(We are) *always carrying in the body the death of Jesus, so that the life of Jesus may also be made visible in our bodies. For while we live, we are always being given up to death for Jesus' sake, so that the life of Jesus may be made visible in our mortal flesh.*[2]

There's a new way of living for the new creation:

- *Love from the center of who you are*
- *Don't fake it*
- *Run for dear life from evil*

---

[1] Romans 6:11
[2] 2 Corinthians 4:10-11 NRSV

- *Hold on for dear life to good.*
- *Be good friends who love deeply*
- *Practice playing second fiddle*
- *Don't burn out*
- *Keep yourselves fueled and aflame*
- *Be alert servants of the Master*
- *Be cheerfully expectant*
- *Don't quit in hard times*
- *Pray all the harder*
- *Help needy Christians*
- *Be inventive in hospitality*
- *Bless your enemies*
- *No cursing under your breath*
- *Laugh with your happy friends when they're happy*
- *Share tears when they're down*
- *Get along with each other*
- *Don't be stuck up*
- *Make friends with nobodies*
- *Don't be the greatest somebody.*
- *Don't hit back*
- *Discover beauty in everyone*

- *If you've got it in you, get along with everybody.*
- *Don't insist on getting even*
- *That's not for you to do*
- *"I'll do the judging," says God*
- *"I'll take care of it."*[3]

Only Holy Spirit-infused believers have the continuous enablement to live according to the *bylaws* of the kingdom.[4] Law for the natural man is typified: *An eye for an eye. Retaliation* is the automatic reaction and response for the Adam man.

Restraint is the disciplined reaction of those who are graced for kingdom rule and response. Here's God's specific and to-the-point command to the Jesus man:

- *That's not for you to do*
- *"I'll do the judging."*
- *"I'll take care of it."*

Here's what follows:

Be a good citizen. All governments are under God. Insofar as there is peace and order, it's God's order. So live responsibly as a citizen. If you're irresponsible to the state,

---

[3] Romans 12:9-21 TM
[4] Matthew 5-7

then you're irresponsible with God, and God will hold you responsible. Duly constituted authorities are only a threat if you're trying to get by with something. Decent citizens should have nothing to fear.[5]

The life of new creation sons of the kingdom should look different than the unbelievers—oh, maybe not on the outside. (We should not draw attention to ourselves by outward appearances.)[6] But, we let our lights shine (our inward parts be revealed) by our attitudes—especially as it pertains to matters of justice and righteousness.

The Holy Spirit will sometimes call upon us to confront injustices and unrighteousness. Our attitudes will reveal the Source (or source) of our confrontations. Remember that *faith works by love*,[7] and that *which is not of faith is sin*.[8]

Retaliation is the overriding necessity of the flesh; love and forgiveness are the overriding virtues of the kingdom.

Retaliation does not translate into justice according to the higher ways of God. *Moderation is better than muscle; self-control better than political power.*[9]

---

[5] Romans 13:1 TM
[6] 1 Corinthians 9:19-23
[7] Galatians 5:6
[8] Romans 14:23
[9] Proverbs 16:32 TM

Chapter 10

Unruly Rudders

A bit in the mouth of a horse controls the whole horse. A small rudder on a huge ship in the hands of a skilled captain sets a course in the face of the strongest winds.

A word out of your mouth may seem of no account, but it can accomplish nearly anything—or destroy it![1]

Dean was a very prophetic young man—lots of potential, but yet immature. He would call me from the West Coast between 5 and 6 a.m. his time, and I would try to encourage him.

His pastor saw him as a problem to be endured. He had no grace for investing in Dean's spiritual upbringing. He just wanted to keep him under control so that his job didn't get even more difficult.

I read some of Dean's writings, and could discern that he truly was a gifted young man. I asked the pastor if he would release him into my care, and he was not willing.

One morning when his wife, Maria, returned from driving the children to school, she smelled something burning. She went to the garage and was horrified to

[1] James 3:3-5 TM

see Dean in flames. He had tied himself to a chair, doused himself with gasoline, and lit the match. Still conscious, he said, "Don't worry about me. Take care of yourself."

There were three suicides in that fellowship within a few years. The pastor was a good man with a good heart and a sincere desire to honor and serve God. But, he was alone, and had a very narrow administrative gifting—a place for everything, and everything in its place. Dean did not fit in his *box*!

Both Leaders and Followers can be Victims of the System

In my fifty years of service to Christ and His people, I have found very few leaders who willingly or intentionally hurt people. I realize that there are some who are very ambitious and building their own kingdoms. But, I can honestly say that—among those whom I have known personally, the fingers on one hand would be adequate for keeping this score. That averages out to one person every ten years. And, I cannot think of five leaders who set out to hurt or destroy people.

Surely those who teach and lead must know that they have a huge responsibility, not just for what they say or teach, but—to some extent—for how they are perceived. Ministry can be misunderstood by anyone--especially spiritually immature people.

Pulpit ministry is often misunderstood by those who stand behind them. There is a difference between broadcasting and communicating. Examination must precede prognosis. Diagnosis must come before prescription.

Would it not be irresponsible for a physician and pharmacist to throw bucketfuls of prescription drugs at a crowd of people, trusting that each one will get the medicine he/she needs?

This is a common error that can be laid at the feet of a religious system that prematurely platforms and promotes people on the basis of charisma rather than character, credentials rather than proven credibility. Ill-prepared people operating in a poorly conceived system do damage to people.

It is not uncommon for emotionally-warped people to find identity is positions of authority. Tragic!

Don't be in any rush to become a teacher, my friends. Teaching is highly responsible work. Teachers are held to the strictest standards.[2]

In spite of this clear warning, so many casually put their opinions on the line—online—for the whole world to view. Facebook and other social and business media offer platforms for "editorializing" about pet peeves as well as pet doctrines.

---

[2] James 3:1 TM

It is easier now than ever to find someone who is saying what you want to hear. Then, all you need to do is click on "Forward" to send it on to influence (or get back at) others.

Death and life are in the power of the tongue, and those who love it will eat its fruit.[3]

This can go either way. It is way too easy to find those who will love and eat the fruit of unrighteous judgment. The Message Bible says it this way:

Words kill, words give life; they're either poison or fruit—you choose.

A Need for Fathering and Mothering

When people come to Christ and to the church as orphans out of an orphan culture and fatherless society, they normally have their share of predispositions and wounds.[4] Both predispositions and wounds have exponentially multiplied in more recent years as the culture around us has deteriorated, and the church world has passively fallen into the same patterns.

---

[3] Proverbs 18:21

[4] What some identify as *wounds* or *abuses* are often nothing more than *predispositions* and *perceptions*. Many bring baggage with them into a given situation that actually prevents them from rightly hearing and seeing. Disillusionment is sometimes a stepping stone toward deliverance, setting an individual free from illusion(s).

Compounding the challenge is the "undone" condition of so many believers who have been neither adequately shepherded nor properly discipled. Consequently, new believers whose sensitivities are still in pain from rejection or abuse are brought into the fellowship of other believers who are in the same condition. And, wounded people wound people.

Many go throughout their entire lives as spiritual babies, not thinking that they are spiritual babies because they have been Christians for many years. You will know them by their fruit.

I have a lot more to say about this, but it is hard to get it across to you since you've picked up this bad habit of not listening. By this time you ought to be teachers yourselves, yet here I find you need someone to sit down with you and go over the basics on God again, starting from square one—baby's milk, when you should have been on solid food long ago! Milk is for beginners, inexperience in God's ways; solid food is for the mature, who have some practice in telling right from wrong.[5]

As stated earlier, many such saints make the mistake of trying to teach others in the free-wheeling cyber world. Compounding this situation are ministers who take up an offense for the offended, rather than encouraging them in the direction of loving discipline and instruction. We should explain to people that standing still and remaining in reaction is not the

---

[5] Hebrews 5:11-14 TM

pathway to wholeness. It is forward movement and the guidance of elder brothers and sisters that will bring them progress.

Shepherding Grace

We need the shepherd grace to bring mending and healing to those who are coming to Christ. This process will not progress in meetings or lectures. There is a great need for one-on-one ministry. We should pray that God would show us how to bring forth and release multiple people—men and women—who have the shepherding anointing.

The healing process proceeds as our Father releases the Balm of Gilead—virtue—from heaven through the words and the hands of others, helping victims to become victors because of the stripes of Jesus, His death, and His subsequent resurrection.

There is also a dying to self that is necessary for the release of newness of life in the power of the Spirit. So many Christians continue unnecessarily in their wounded and self-guarded condition for the lack of adequate shepherding, or lack of willingness to be vulnerable again.

Regardless of your role—leader or follower—we are challenged to bring our rudder (our tongue) under the loving lordship of Christ.

This is scary. You can tame a tiger, but you can't tame a tongue—it's never been done. The tongue runs wild, a wanton killer. With our tongues we bless God our Father; with the same tongues we curse the very men and women He made in His image. Curses and blessings out of the same mouth!

My friends, this can't go on. A spring doesn't gush fresh water one day and brackish water the next, does it? Apple trees don't bear strawberries, do they? Raspberry bushes don't bear apples, do they? You're not going to dip into a polluted mud hole and get a cup of clear, cool water, are you?[6]

Here is Jesus' promise:

"If anyone thirsts, let him come to Me and drink. Rivers of living water will brim and spill out of the depths of anyone who believes in Me this way."[7]

Key: You must consider yourself dead to live His life!

---

[6] James 3:7-12 TM
[7] John 7:37-38 TM

Chapter 11

Loose Your Grip

Seems like a contradiction. Did we not write about "Loving Life" and "Fighting to Live?" I do not advocate losing your grip. I am suggesting that you loose your grip. Loose, not lose!

The life of which we write—*the life which we now live in the flesh we live by faith in the Son of God, who loved us and gave Himself for us*—is in His hands, not ours.

Contradiction to the unrenewed mind? Yes, but not a contradiction to the heart that is at peace with our Father. No white-knuckled choke holds on the self-life.

"Our friends are facing the giant of cancer. Esther is riddled with the death cells. As we visited in their living room, Esther sat, contentment softening the lines of her face as she smiled and said, 'I want God to heal me for His glory, but if this is the time I am supposed to leave the earth, I am ready and at peace and content.' She then said, 'Gene will be all right; God will take care of him, but I am ready to go and ready to stay, it's all in the Lord's hands.'

"I know many who would call Esther's position a lack of faith, that she is inviting death. I see her position as the ultimate expression of true faith in a Father Who does all things well."[1]

Of the increase of His government and peace there will be no end.[2]

Isaiah was prompted to identify "peace" as the *by-product* or *fruit* of His government, acknowledging that both His *government* and His *peace* continually increase together. Peace is the evidence/testimony of being in His will.

My heart goes out to those who—filled with tons of anxiety—challenge those who are at peace, that "they do not have faith!" It is wearying work to invest great effort into living by *presumption, principles,* and *proof texts.*

While life is to be rightly valued, believers are to have a handle on the unseen:

The fundamental fact of existence is that this trust in God, this faith, is the firm foundation under everything that makes life worth living. It's our handle on what we can't see. The act of faith is what distinguished our ancestors, set them above the crowd.[3]

---

[1] Greg Austin
[2] Isaiah 9:7
[3] Hebrews 11:1-2 TM

The Hebrew writer continued with many testimonies that are parts of our heritage as sons of God. Reading through chapter eleven, we find those who *escaped the edge of the sword*[4] and others who were *slain with the sword.*[5]

Both those who escaped and those who did not are mentioned within the context of men and women of faith.

A Perspective on Faith

Faith is not a ticket for our personal and physical well-being. Faith believes. Faith trusts. Faith surrenders all control to our Father in heaven. (This is, in itself, presumption. Perhaps it would be more accurate to say that we acknowledge and willingly affirm and embrace His control as the very best thing for us.)

He has taken the sting out of death, and removed the victory from the grave. In resurrection power, He has conquered the last enemy!

Inasmuch then as the children have partaken of flesh and blood, He Himself likewise shared in the same, that through death He might destroy him who had the power of death,

---

[4] Hebrews 11:34
[5] Hebrews 11:37

that is the devil, and release those who through fear of death were all their lifetime subject to bondage.[6]

You name the particular bondage, and I'll draw the line for you directly to the fear of death! The devil holds many saints in the grip of bondage because they fear death. This is because people believe lies! Through death, Jesus destroyed him who had the power of death. Release is ours in Jesus's name!

Let me tell you something wonderful, a mystery I'll probably never fully understand. We're not all going to die—but we are all going to be changed. You hear a blast to end all blasts from a trumpet, and in the time that you look up and blink your eyes—it's over. On signal from the trumpet from heaven, the dead will be up and out of their graves, beyond the reach of death, never to die again. At the same moment and in the same way, we'll all be changed. In the resurrection scheme of things, this has to happen: everything perishable taken off the shelves and replaced by the imperishable, this mortal replaced by the immortal. Then the saying will come true:

> *Death swallowed by triumphant Life!*
> *Who got the last word, oh, Death?*
> *Oh, Death, who's afraid of you now?*[7]

---

[6] Hebrews 2:14-15
[7] 1 Corinthians 15:51-55 TM

Ready for an Adventure

Confidence in the Word of God, witnessed to us by the Spirit of God, frees us now from the fear of death and empowers us to slip out of the chains of bondage in any form. To know that we are eternally kept, that our destiny is secure in the palm of Father's hand, releases us to a level of adventurous living previously unimaginable to any responsible mind.

Take a little time to inquire of God. Is this true? Is the fact that the grave could not hold Jesus evidence that the grave will not hold us? It seems that, in a very real way, we are already enjoying so many aspects of resurrection life. We already enjoy the *firstfruits of the Spirit.* Only our mortal bodies need to be replaced by immortality, and the process of adoption will be absolutely complete![8]

Paul got it! Paul lived it!

For we know that if our earthly house, this tent, is destroyed, we have a building from God, a house not made with hands, eternal in the heavens. For in this we groan, earnestly desiring to be clothed with our habitation which is from heaven, if indeed having been clothed, we shall not be found naked.

---

[8] Romans 8:23

For we who are in this tent groan, being burdened, not because we want to be unclothed, but further clothed, that mortality may be swallowed up by life.

Now He who has prepared us for this very thing is God, who also has given us the Spirit as a guarantee. So we are always confident, knowing that while we are at home in the body we are absent from the Lord.

For we walk by faith, not by sight. We are confident, yes, well pleased rather to be absent from the body and to be present with the Lord. Therefore we make it our aim, whether present or absent, to be well pleasing to Him.[9]

You and I can live in this confidence and walk in this faith. We are the benefactors of *the firstfruits of the Spirit, the guarantee. Let the peace of God rule in your hearts.*[10]

To settle the death issue is the most freeing thing you can do in your preparation to live life in Him!

---

[9] 2 Corinthians 5:1-9
[10] Colossians 3:15

Chapter 12

Free From Yesterday

Letting go of yesterday begins by letting go of the *old man*.

Speaking many years ago in a church in Brockport, New York, I asked a young man from the congregation to come forward. He was about my height, but (strategically) not my weight. I had him stand behind me, putting his arms over my shoulders. I took hold of his hands, and tipping lightly forward, lifted him off his feet. He was suspended on my back and I was carrying the whole load of his body.

Struggling under the weight, I slowly went across the front of the auditorium, turned, and returned to the other side.

"That is the way that many Christians live their lives! They continue to carry the dead cadaver of their *old man* on their backs, day in and day out, and wonder why they are not making more progress in their walk in Christ!"

That illustration proved to set many people free that day.

Could it be any clearer? Our old way of life was nailed to the cross with Christ, a decisive end to that sin-miserable life—no longer at sin's every beck and call! What we believe is this: If we get included in Christ's sin-conquering death, we also get included in His life-saving resurrection. Never again will death have the last word.[1]

Hallelujah! In Christ, we are free to learn new ways of living. Because in Him, we have risen to walk in newness of life.

This mystery has been kept in the dark for a long time, but now it's out in the open. God wanted everyone, not just Jews, to know this rich and glorious secret inside out, regardless of their background, regardless of their religious standing. The mystery in a nutshell is just this:

Christ is in you, so therefore you can look forward to sharing in God's glory. It's that simple.[2]

Newness of Life

Your background has no influence on your foreground! Your background had everything to do with an old man who was buried with Christ; your foreground has everything to do with a new species, a new creation.

---

[1] Romans 6:6-9 TM
[2] Colossians 1:26-27 TM

Therefore, if anyone is in Christ, he is a new creation; old things have passed away; behold all things have become new.[3]

When we look around us with our natural eyes, still considering our situation and condition according to our natural understanding, all things appear to be the same old things, the same old situation, and the same old condition.

There is a huge difference! There is an entirely new root system and power supply that is already initiating significant changes. As we are being *transformed by the renewing of our minds,*[4] we begin to realize:

- All that I used to be guilty of has been washed away.
- All that I used to be in bondage to has lost its power.
- All that I ever dreamed about has no more allure.
- Suddenly, I am experiencing new dreams and different visions.

---

[3] 2 Corinthians 5:17
[4] Romans 12:2

- Impossibilities have become possibilities.

- It is no longer about me.

- It is no longer up to me.

- I am the benefactor of power from on high.

Brethren, I do not count myself to have apprehended; but one thing I do, forgetting those things which are behind and reaching forward to those things which are ahead, I press toward the goal for the prize of the upward call of God in Christ Jesus.[5]

[5] Philippians 3:12-14

Chapter 13

Trust For Tomorrow

"Don't be afraid of tomorrow—God is already there."[1]

"Give your entire attention to what God is doing right now, and don't get worked up about what may or may not happen tomorrow. God will help you deal with whatever hard things come up when the time comes."[2]

On several occasions, our Father has guided us to give our last ten dollars away. That's tough—especially when you have the responsibilities that go along with having children. Living life on the cutting edge of faith truly helps us to die daily!

Our last regular salary ended early in June 1968. Many seasons have followed. With Paul, we have contentment.

I know how to be abased, and I know how to abound. Everywhere and in all things I have learned both to be full and to be hungry, both to abound and to suffer need. I can do all things through Christ who strengthens me.[3]

---

[1] Unknown
[2] Matthew 6:34 TM
[3] Philippians 4:12-13

Life on the Cutting Edge

Believers find the riches of God's kingdom on the cutting edge. You can choose to live as though you have no salary, simply gratefully receiving it as part of God's provision for you. That way, you are already conditioned by faith for our Father to change the channel of supply or supplement as you steward everything that comes to your hand as His.

The cutting edge is the *growing* edge. That's where the pruning takes place. No pruning—no increase in fruitfulness!

"I am the Real Vine and My Father is the Farmer. He cuts off every branch of Me that doesn't bear grapes. And every branch that is grape-bearing He prunes back so it will bear even more."[4]

The writer of the Epistle to the Hebrews makes it quite clear:

The fundamental fact of existence is that this trust in God, this faith, is the firm foundation under everything that makes life worth living. It's our handle on what we can't see.[5]

---

[4] John 15:1-2 TM

[5] Hebrews 11:1-2 TM

Every time we gave away our last ten dollars God paid it back within hours! (Don't go giving away anything without God's telling you to!)

The most obvious challenge to the faith of most people involves material possessions or personal safety. Today's orphan culture is primarily concerned about provision and protection. The slave mentality doesn't trust anyone. But, sons can trust their Father! God is the Master provider and protector.

With God on our side like this, how can we lose?[6]

Regardless of the acts of men and angels, we can be secure.

I'm absolutely convinced that nothing—nothing living or dead, angelic or demonic, today or tomorrow, high or low, thinkable or unthinkable—absolutely nothing can get between us and God's love because of the way that Jesus our Master has embraced us.[7]

Read my lips! No one or no thing can interfere with your becoming what God created you to be. However, if you fall subject to rejection, rebellion, hurt, woundedness, anger, bitterness, and the like, you have marginalized your destiny by your own

---

[6] Romans 8:31 TM
[7] Romans 8:39 TM

carnality. Fear is the antithesis of faith. *The righteous will live by faith.*[8]

Your Position and Responsibilities in Christ

If you are in Christ, then anything that gets to you had to come through Christ to get to you. That is, whatever comes to you does so with His permission. And, He promises that He *will not allow you to be tempted beyond what you are able, but with the temptation will also make the way of escape, that you may be able to bear it.*[9] Key: Learning to lean on Jesus in very practical ways. His life and strength within us is His provided way of escape.

My brethren, count it all joy when you fall into various trials, knowing that the testing of your faith produces patience. But let patience have its perfect work, that you may be perfect and complete, lacking nothing.[10]

The way of escape is often:

- Humbling ourselves
- Asking forgiveness
- Forgiving others

Trust God with other people. Release them. If you hang onto an offense, you are attempting to do God's

---

[8] Romans 1:17
[9] 1 Corinthians 10:13
[10] James 1:2-4

part. When you release them, God's wholeness is available to you, and He is free to do the right thing for the others involved.

We expect babies to grow into responsible adults. Yet, in the spiritual realm, many people spend their entire lives in the nursery. It does not matter how many years you have been a Christian, you are not going to grow into your destiny while holding bitterness and/or unforgiveness in your heart.

So long as there are divisions among you, you are yet carnal.[11] We cannot conduct ourselves like mere men and grow into God's ultimate intention.

Trust is the issue. Trusting God with others as well as trusting Him for our own tomorrows is the key that unlocks the kingdom for us.

"If you grasp and cling to life on your terms, you'll lose it, but if you let that life go, you'll get life on God's terms."[12]

---

[11] 1 Corinthians 3:3
[12] Luke 17:33 TM

Chapter 14

The "Quickening" Factor

And if Christ be in you, the body is dead because of sin; but the spirit is life because of righteousness.

But if the Spirit of Him that raised up Jesus from the dead dwell in you, He that raised up Christ from the dead shall also quicken your mortal bodies by His Spirit that dwelleth in you.[1]

We were walking and talking dead men at one time. And then we were born again by the Spirit of the living God. He raised Jesus in an immortal body in order that we might know what to expect—eventually.

In the meantime, the same Spirit that raised Jesus in His immortal body also quickens our mortal bodies! Let's slow down and look at this in the Amplified Version:

But if Christ lives in you, [then although] your [natural] body is dead by reasons of sin and guilt, the spirit is alive because of [the] righteousness [that He imputes to you].

[1] Romans 8:10-11 KJV

And if the Spirit of Him Who raised up Jesus from the dead dwells in you, [then] He Who raised up Christ Jesus from the dead will also restore to life your mortal (short-lived, perishable) bodies through His Spirit Who dwells in you.[2]

It was His higher thought and His higher way[3] to impute unto us His righteousness.[4] And, while we wait for the *twinkling* that will dress us in immortality, in the meantime, the Spirit of life in Christ Jesus gives life to our mortal bodies!

The implications of this truth are mind-boggling! Our faith can be significantly elevated by simply getting this truth into our spirits, past all of the barriers, barbed wire and quicksand in the mind.

"As you go, preach, saying 'The kingdom of heaven is at hand.' Heal the sick, cleanse the lepers, raise the dead, cast out demons. Freely you have received, freely give."[5]

"These signs will follow those who believe: In My name they will cast out demons; they will speak with new tongues; they will take up serpents; and if they drink anything deadly, it will by no means hurt them; they will lay hands on the sick, and they will recover."[6]

---

[2] Romans 8:10-11 AMP

[3] Isaiah 55:8

[4] To attribute (righteousness, guilt, etc.) to a person or persons vicariously; ascribe as derived from another.

[5] Matthew 10:7-8

[6] Mark 16:17-18

I am not suggesting that we can perform *charismagic* miracles based upon proof texts. But, what I am saying is that the Spirit of God within us can do what He wishes with what He created. He can fix what is broken, replace what is missing, re-order what is out of line, and bring back life to what has died. He always has spare parts in His toolbox, and He is always with us.

He is the Master of the molecular. He can change chemistry. Nothing is impossible for Him, and nothing is impossible for us as we learn to live in rightful union in Him—desiring only to obey and glorify Him.

The Spirit of *Christ in* us *is the hope of glory.*[7] He said:

"Most assuredly I say to you, he who believes in Me, the works that I do he will do also; and greater works than these he will do, because I go to My Father."[8]

Jesus intimated rather openly that His disciples would do greater works that what He had done. What he had done was the fruit of His abiding with the Father, and His singleness of eye to see and do only what He saw His Father doing. He laid out such a pattern for us!

---

[7] Colossians 1:27
[8] John 14:12

On a single day, the day of Pentecost, Jesus' disciples cumulatively did more. Jesus was not surprised. The schematic blueprint was a part of Him, even as it is a part of true apostles today.

We would also see the "greater works" if we were able to measure and record the cumulative work of His Spirit through His disciples globally.

We have personally witnessed the deaf hearing, the dumb speaking, the blind seeing, and the lame walking—*walking and leaping, and praising God!*[9] We have seen limbs grow, deformities disappear, demoniacs clothed and in their right minds.

Severe deterioration of the lower back left my wife immobile and wracked with pain—until God delivered her from spirits of infirmity and pain, and gave her a new back (confirmed by x-ray). A sty in each eye of one of our daughters instantly disappeared.

These are just a few of the many examples of what we have been privileged to see and experience for ourselves.

Yet, our daughter, Diane, died.

---

[9] Acts 3:8

Where was God then?

He was outfitting her with immortality, while at the same time comforting us, increasing our trust in Him, and taking us from glory to glory.

Chapter 15

Living in View of Eternity

Dear reader, my intention is that, by now, we have established an atmosphere of faith by immersing ourselves in what the Scripture has to say regarding issues of life and death.

We have come far enough together now to really level with one another regarding the most difficult of difficulties. I am not suggesting that you put your head in the sand. I am not asking you to walk in denial. There are certain certainties that accompany our walk together in Christ. There are inevitable inevitabilities that we cannot hurdle or find a way around.

Physical death is most evident, but not necessarily imminent for all who are reading this. The early believers expected the culmination of all things during their lifetime. That was more than two thousand years ago!

A variety of crazy eschatology has emerged over the years—especially in the past two centuries. I'm not smart enough to figure it all out. But, this is among the certain certainties, the inevitable inevitabilities:

Everyone has to die once, then face the consequences. Christ's death was also a one-time event, but it was a sacrifice that took care of sins forever. And so, when He next appears, the outcome for those eager to greet Him is, precisely, salvation.[1]

Get it? Let's say it another way:

And as it is appointed for men to die once, but after this the judgment, so Christ was offered once to bear the sins of many. To those who eagerly wait for Him He will appear a second time, apart from sin, for salvation.[2]

"I will not leave you orphaned. I'm coming back. In just a little while the world will no longer see Me, but you're going to see Me because I am alive and you're about to come alive."[3]

Christ's Spirit within us is a down payment on our inheritance, the assurance of our eternal participation in His kingdom and glory!

Jesus said: *"The world will no longer see Me, but you're going to see Me."* The writer of Hebrews promised that "He will appear to those who eagerly wait for Him."

---

[1] Hebrews 9:27-28 TM
[2] Hebrews 9:27-28 NKJV
[3] John 14:18-19 TM

Aspects of the kingdom of heaven in the earth have been introduced ever since Adam blew it. Christ was the initial investment of the kingdom into the earth. His planting has resulted in sons of the kingdom being scattered throughout the earth in every previous generation.

The sowing of our lives into the kingdom on earth will produce a great harvest in which we will participate. It will be inaugurated in the twinkling of an eye.

He thought of everything, provided for everything we could possibly need, letting us in on the plans He took such delight in making. He set it all out before us in Christ, a long-range plan in which everything would be brought together and summed up in Him, everything in deepest heaven, everything on planet earth.

The dead in Christ will rise first.

Then we who are alive and remain shall be caught up together with them in the clouds to meet the Lord in the air. And thus we shall always be with the Lord.

It may be like a child running down the sidewalk to meet his dad coming home, taking his hand, and excitedly walking with him back to our house!

Therefore, comfort one another with these words.[4]

---

[4] 1 Thessalonians 4:13-18

We can take comfort even when meted out to us in allegories, metaphors, parables, and types and shadows. Hopefully, even reading this book brings comfort and assurance.

Unraveling Mysteries Comes by Permission

Jesus was questioned as to why He used parables. The mysteries of the kingdom are often discerned at heart level by His disciples, while remaining hidden from others.

God's wisdom is something mysterious that goes deep into the interior of His purposes. You don't find it lying around on the surface.[5]

I actually pray that you will NOT draw any doctrinal conclusions regarding the consummation of all things in Christ. Your chances of getting it right are relatively minimal. Your chances of thinking that you know will most certainly be counterproductive.

In that moment when all things—things in heaven, and things in earth—are consummated in Christ, we will all see clearly. In the meantime, we must settle to see dimly. We will be limited by our mortality until it is exchanged for immortality.

---

[5] 1 Corinthians 2:6 TM

It is inevitable that our ideas and opinions—even when presented as dogma—fall short of the glory of God.

Living in view of eternity is not the result of personal study or intellectual conclusion. Living in view of eternity is the fruit of faith that comes by hearing (or reading).[6]

Paul lived in view of eternity. He instructed Timothy:

Be watchful in all things, endure afflictions, do the work of an evangelist, fulfill your ministry. For I am already being poured out as a drink offering, and the time of my departure is at hand. I have fought the good fight. I have finished the race, I have kept the faith.

Finally, there is laid up for me the crown of righteousness, which the Lord, the righteous Judge, will give to me on that Day, and not to me only but also to all who have loved His appearing.[7]

Have you loved His appearing? Remember His promise just before His crucifixion?

"I will not leave you orphaned. I'm coming back. In just a little while the world will no longer see Me, but you're going to see Me because I am alive and you're about to come alive."

---

[6] Romans 10:17
[7] 2 Timothy 4:5-8

Chapter 16

Cloudless Heavens

When I speak of Cloudless Heavens, I am not prophesying a lack of rain! Nor am I suggesting a problem-free life.

"Indeed the hour is coming, yes, has now come, that you will be scattered, each to his own, and will leave Me alone. And yet I am not alone, because the Father is with Me. These things I have spoken to you, that in Me you may have peace. In the world you will have tribulation, but be of good cheer, I have overcome the world."[8]

Rain will come. Life will have its storms. When I speak of cloudless heavens, I'm talking about *perspective!* From where are you looking? How and where do you see and understand your position?

Salvation and power are established!
  Kingdom of God, authority of His Messiah!
The Accuser of our brothers and sisters thrown out,
  who accused them day and night before God.
They defeated him through the blood of the Lamb
  And the bold word of their witness.
They weren't in love with themselves;
  they were willing to die for Christ.

---

[8] John 16:32-33

So rejoice, O Heavens, and all who live there,
But doom to earth and sea,
For the Devil's come down on you with both feet;
he's had a great fall;
He's wild and raging with anger;
he hasn't much time and he knows it.[9]

Those who *have been raised up together and made to sit together in heavenly places in Christ Jesus*[10] can rejoice!

"Heaven is My throne, and earth is My footstool."[11]

We look down upon those things that non-believers look up to see. Our perspective in view of eternity is totally different. We rejoice at what is doom to them.

"We can do this! The Spirit of our Father is with us. We are never alone. Jesus' Spirit is one with the Father's Spirit. There is a day coming soon when we will prove to be the benefactors of a better covenant. We are a new species—a new creation.

Oneness

"The Spirit of our Father, is one with our spirits, and we will overcome the world. We will rescue and restore the creation back to its original beauty and productivity.

---

[9] Revelation 12:10-12 TM
[10] Ephesians 2:6
[11] Acts 7:49a. Also consider Hebrews 2:5-11

"Even now the heavens are without clouds to those who are seated in heavenly places and have eyes to see. Even seeing dimly, we have the full advantage and accurate perspective of looking down from where we are seated in Him."[12]

Why would someone who is seated in the heavenlies need a *portal,* a place of access, into heaven?

If then you were raised with Christ, seek those things which are above, where Christ is sitting at the right hand of God. Set your mind on things above, not on things on the earth.

We have died, and our lives are hidden with Christ in God. When Christ who is our life appears, then we will also appear with Him in glory. Therefore, put to death your members which are on the earth.[13]

Make it your faith perspective to view everything from our vantage point with Christ on the throne of His father David. Get in the habit! Become accustomed to having this point of view.

To the extent that you walk in this reality the transition that will take place in the twinkling of an eye may go almost unnoticed.

Time and space are limiting factors primarily for the unbelievers. That's how Paul could say, *For I indeed,*

---

[12] Prophetic insight; Ephesians 2:4-7
[13] Colossians 3:1-5a

as absent in body but present in spirit, have already judged (as though I were present) him who has so done this deed.[14]

"The kingdom of God does not come by observation; nor will they say, 'See here!' or 'See there!' For indeed, the kingdom of God is within you."[15]

Let us therefore come boldly to the throne of grace, that we may obtain mercy and find grace to help in time of need.[16]

We are graced for the smoothest and quickest of transitions—like going to sleep and waking up in an upgrade, with the greatest of makeovers – incorrupt immortality!

In your ocean, I'm ankle deep
I feel the waves crashin' on my feet
It's like I know where I need to be
But I can't figure out, yeah I can't figure out

Just how much air I will need to breathe
When your tide rushes over me
There's only one way to figure out
Will ya let me drown, will ya let me drown

Hey now, this is my desire
Consume me like a fire, 'cause I just want something beautiful

[14] 1 Corinthians 5:3
[15] Luke 17:20-21
[16] Hebrews 4:16

To touch me, I know that I'm in reach
'Cause I am down on my knees, I'm waiting for something beautiful
Oh, something beautiful

And the water is risin' quick
And for years I was scared of it
We can't be sure when it will subside
So I won't leave your side, no I can't leave your side

Hey now, this is my desire
Consume me like a fire, 'cause I just want something beautiful
To touch me, I know that I'm in reach
'Cause I am down on my knees, I'm waiting for something beautiful
Oh, something beautiful

In a daydream, I couldn't live like this
I wouldn't stop until I found something beautiful
When I wake up, and all I want, I have
You know its still not what I need
Something beautiful

Hey now, this is my desire
Consume me like a fire, 'cause I just want something beautiful
To touch me, I know that I'm in reach
'Cause I am down on my knees, I'm waiting for

something beautiful
Oh, something beautiful[17]

[17] NeedToBreathe

Chapter 17

Something Beautiful

If there ever were dreams
That were lofty and noble
They were my dreams at the start
And hope for life's best were the hopes
That I harbor down deep in my heart
But my dreams turned to ashes
And my castles all crumbled,
My fortune turned to loss
So I wrapped it all in the rags of life
And laid it at the cross.

Something beautiful, something good
All my confusion He understood
All I had to offer Him was brokenness and strife
But he made something beautiful of my life.[1]

As It Is In Heaven

The kingdom of God on the earth is beautiful beyond description. And so are we!

I saw Heaven and earth new-created. Gone the first Heaven, gone the first earth, gone the sea. I saw Holy

[1] Gaither

Jerusalem, new-created, descending resplendent out of Heaven, as ready for God as a bride for her husband.

I heard a voice thunder from the Throne: "Look! Look! God has moved into the neighborhood, making His home with men and women! They're His people, He's their God.

He'll wipe every tear from their eyes. Death is gone for good—tears gone, crying gone, pain gone—all the first order of things gone." The enthroned continued, "Look! I'm making everything new. Write it all down—each word dependable and accurate."

Then He said, "It's happened. I'm A to Z. I'm the Beginning, I'm the Conclusion. From Water-of-Life Well I give freely to the thirsty. Conquerors inherit all this. I'll be God to them, they'll be sons and daughters to Me."[2]

Paul obviously lived life in the Spirit, living in view of eternity. Here's how he described his old life in Adam:

- Circumcised the eighth day
- Of the stock of Israel
- Of the tribe of Benjamin
- A Hebrew of Hebrews
- A Pharisee

---

[2] Revelation 21:1-7 TM

- Zealous
- Persecuted the church
- Righteous
- Blameless

What things were gain to me, these I have counted as loss for Christ. Yet indeed I also count all things loss for the excellence of the knowledge of Christ Jesus my Lord, for whom I have suffered the loss of all things, and count them as rubbish, that I may gain Christ and be found in Him, not having my own righteousness, which is from the law, but that which is through faith in Christ, the righteous which is from God by faith; that I may know Him and the power of His resurrection, and the fellowship of His sufferings, being conformed to His death, if by any means, I may attain to the resurrection from the dead.[3]

Paul was gloriously converted on the road to Damascus. He exchanged all of his worldly successes and failures, was crucified with Christ, and lived the life of Christ within him through the Power of the Holy Spirit. Here are some of his significant proclamations:

- To live is Christ
- To die is gain
- To be absent from the body

---

[3] Philippians 3:7-11

- To be present with the Lord
- I am hard-pressed between the two
- Having a desire to depart and be with Christ which is far better
- Nevertheless to remain in the flesh is more needful for you

Having developed a keen awareness of the realities that are just a breath beyond human touch, Paul knew what was better—something beautiful. But, he was overwhelmed and overruled by Christ in him, the hope of glory, and chose to complete his course, run his race responsibly. And, thereby glorify God on the earth.

Jesus said,

"I have glorified You on the earth. I have finished the work which You have given Me to do.

"And now, O Father, glorify Me together with Yourself, with the glory which I had with You before the world was."[4]

The life that we have known in this time-space world is only an interlude in eternity.

---

[4] John 17:4-5

Chapter 18

I Can Face Tomorrow

God sent His son, they called Him, Jesus;
He came to love, heal and forgive;
He lived and died to buy my pardon,
An empty grave is there to prove my Savior lives!

Because He lives, I can face tomorrow,
Because He lives, all fear is gone;
Because I know He holds the future,
And life is worth the living,
Just because He lives!

How sweet to hold a newborn baby,
And feel the pride and joy he gives;
But greater still the calm assurance:
This child can face uncertain days because He Lives!

And then one day, I'll cross the river,
I'll fight life's final war with pain;
And then, as death gives way to vict'ry,
I'll see the lights of glory and I'll know He lives![1]

---

[1] Gaither

As It Is In Heaven

The kingdom on earth—if you can imagine—will be filled with God's order and its corresponding peace. Love will rule; joy will be resplendent.

The great distance between *the Lion of the tribe of Judah,* and *the Lamb that takes away the sins of the world,* will virtually evaporate as—metaphorically--the Lion in Jesus lays down with the Lamb in Jesus, in total oneness. When we see this we will know for sure that we have the mind of Christ—and see as He sees.

Our perspective of Jesus limits both our understanding and our responses. Some can see Him only as the Lion, while others can see Him only as the Lamb. He never stops being both.

Because He lives in us within the fallen cosmos, He grants us the privilege of being what we need to be in the moment. Our service to others requires us to reveal the Lion at times and the Lamb at other times—just as He did in His earthly ministry.

When time is no more, such apparent contradictions that are necessitated by darkness will disappear in the fullness of His light.

"The wolf will romp with the lamb, the leopard sleep with the kid. Calf and lion will eat from the same trough, and a little child shall tend them. Cow and bear will graze the

same pasture, their calves and cubs grow up together, and the lion eat straw like the ox.

"The nursing child will crawl over rattlesnake dens, the toddler stick his hand down the hole of a serpent. Neither animal nor human will hurt or kill on My holy mountain. The whole earth will be brimming with knowing God-Alive, a living knowledge of God ocean-deep, ocean-wide."[2]

"So you'll go out in joy, you'll be led into a whole and complete life. The mountains and hills will lead the parade, bursting with song.

"All the trees of the forest will join the procession, exuberant with applause. No more thistles, but giant sequoias, no more thornbushes, but stately pines, monuments to Me, to God, living and lasting evidence of God."[3]

Perfect everything, everywhere and all the time!

Once again, our God and Father will step back, look over everything He has made, and see that it is good.

Then the Angel showed me Water-of-Life River, crystal bright. It flowed from the Throne of God and the Lamb, right down the middle of the street. The Tree of Life was planted on each side of the River, producing twelve kinds of

---

[2] Isaiah 11:6-9 TM
[3] Isaiah 55:12-13 TM

fruit, a ripe fruit each month. The leaves of the Tree are for healing the nations. Never again will anything be cursed.

The Throne of God and of the Lamb is at the center, His servants will offer God service—worshiping, they'll look on His face, their foreheads mirroring God. Never again will there be any night. No one will need lamplight or sunlight. The shining of God, the Master, is all the light anyone needs.

And they will rule with Him age after age after age.[4]

---

[4] Revelation 11:1-5 TM

Appendix 1

Practical Readiness

My ninety-seven-year-old dad has had prepaid arrangements for the cremation of his body dating back at least thirty years. He has kept me abreast of finances, and anything else that I may need to know—someday—for as long as I remember. I am on his accounts, have power of attorney, and have both his will and living will in my possession.

I have been handling all of his matters for several years. I lived for many years of my life within the confidence of him being there for me. Now, he is secure knowing that I am there for him.

I prayed, asking Father what Dad's purpose is for living such a long life. I knew immediately that Dad was still living for me.

Within days, two people, independent from one another, shared with me Dad's response when they offered to do something or get something for him. He simply said:

"My son will do that; my son will get that for me; my son will take care of that!"

I immediately understood what God meant when He told me that Dad is living for me. Our relationship pictures the fullness of the kingdom!

Our Father is bringing many sons to glory. I can hear it now:

"My son(s) will take care of that!"

Being in Christ provides full coverage for our readiness. However, there are some practical matters concerning those we leave behind which need to be addressed.

I had mentioned earlier that we are uniquely positioned to serve as our generation's *Jacob's ladder*.

We are seated together in the heavens in Christ at the right hand of God. We are also His present-day incarnation available on terra firma for the good of all people. The Holy Spirit allows us to participate in His intercession as He burdens our hearts and reveals His insights and will. We are, from time to time, sent to intervene with the "goods" gained as we intercede.

By virtue of His life and power within, we have the capacity to be very responsible citizens—citizens of the kingdom that is coming in the earth as we speak.

Others ought to be amazed at how we conduct our affairs, impressed enough to ask questions that open doors for kingdom conversations.

There are also fiscal responsibilities that should be taken care of prior to any major transition:

- Do you have a will?
- Is it up to date?
- Have you appointed an administrator?
- Have you appointed a power of attorney?
- Do you have a living will?
- Is someone able to sign on your accounts?
- Is someone apprised of financial matters?
- What about details following your death?
- Is there a plan for final expenses?

Be both thoughtful and prayerful regarding these matters so that you make this final transition as easy as possible for others.

For we know that if our earthly house, this tent, is destroyed, we have a building from God, a house not made with hands, eternal in the heavens.[1]

We know that the whole creation groans and labors with birth pangs together until now. Not only that, but we also who have the firstfruits of the Spirit, even we ourselves groan within ourselves, eagerly waiting for the adoption, the redemption of our body.[2]

There is one glory of the sun, another glory of the moon, and another glory of the stars; for one star differs from another star in glory.

So also is the resurrection of the dead. The body is sown in corruption, it is raised in incorruption. It is sown in dishonor, it is raised in glory. It is sown in weakness, it is raised in power.

It is sown a natural body, it is raised a spiritual body. There is a natural body, and there is a spiritual body.

And so it is written, "The first man Adam became a living being." The last Adam became a life-giving spirit. However, the spiritual is not first, but the natural, and afterward the spiritual.

The first man was from the earth, made of dust; the second Man is the Lord from Heaven. As was the man of dust, so

---

[1] 2 Corinthians 5:1
[2] Romans 8:22-23

also are those who are made of dust; and as is the heavenly Man, so also are those who are heavenly.

And as we have borne the image of the man of dust, we shall also bear the image of the heavenly Man.

Now this I say, brethren, that flesh and blood cannot inherit the kingdom of God; nor does corruption inherit incorruption.

Behold, I tell you a mystery: We shall not all sleep, but we shall all be changed—in a moment, in the twinkling of an eye . . .[3]

"I would like to be taller, thinner, with broad shoulders and narrow waistline. I would like lots of hair.

"But, then, it might not be like that at all. I'm sure that whatever You decide will be perfect for me!"

---

[3] 1 Corinthians 15:41-52a

Appendix 2

A Confirming Email

Dan Hubbell[1]

Don, I just completed reading "Delighted to Die" including the new chapter, "Acquainted With Grief", and want you to know that I confirm and affirm what you have written, my dear brother!

As I read your manuscript, memories flooded my thoughts of similar life experiences about which you wrote in your manuscript.

But to the point that you had mentioned my battle with cancer as your reason for asking my perspective and discernment about this book. So, let me share briefly, that as I faced the diagnosis of cancer and the prognosis of at best of a lengthy recovery, the Lord ministered to me by His grace in several experiences:

1) Background: The first symptom of my having cancer occurred while I was on mission in India. I was led by the Spirit to gather servants from seven nations to meet in India for equipping and mentoring. It was during this gathering that I had to be taken to the hospital

---

[1] www.Church Restoration.org

emergency room to have a catheter put in to relieve the excruciating pain (as you described in your manuscript). A team of us had already been to the Philippines and Indonesia with the intention of concluding our mission with a trip to China. I had to cancel my China leg of the mission, (with my encouragement, the team went on without me), and make arrangements to return to home. With untold effort, I tried to arrange my return flight back as soon as I could. But the earliest arrangement I could make to return was two weeks. The Lord led me to have the trainees to come to my room while I taught them from my bedside with a catheter hanging down. Also, while training these young servants, I received a message from home that my sister had passed away (83 years old). With a catheter at my side and the death message of my sister's death and home going, I taught for an additional two weeks from my bed. After the two weeks of training, I returned home with one of our missionary companions accompanying me.

2) God's ability and power to heal me from cancer was not even in question. I knew He was able, as the three Hebrew children proclaimed, and I had the joy of believing and obeying His word in calling for the elders (James 5:14-16) of the church (whole Body of Christ in our town) to come to our home and

pray over me, anointing me with oil in the name of the Lord. There were seventeen elders from various denominations, including black congregations as well as household congregations, who came to minister to Laurel me in our time of need.

3) I have found over the years that there must be a balance in determining, by the Holy Spirit's discernment, what kind of sickness a person has: Sickness unto healing and/or sickness unto death (to be differentiated from "sin unto unto death"). It takes the whole Body, including the sick person as well as others ministering within their gifting to help discern how to pray within the will of God. And of course the sovereignty and eternal purposes of God must always be uppermost in this ministry. Thus we must always "hear what the Father is saying and see what He is doing" in each situation.

   This distinction can be seen in the various Scriptural examples, i.e., Peter was delivered from death and Stephen and James were martyred; Paul had a "thorn in the flesh" and God's grace was sufficient; Timothy was counseled to take wine for his stomach sake; Paul left Trophimus sick in Miletum; Epaphroditus was sick unto death; etc.

4) Let me illustrate this from one of many experiences on the mission field, but I limit this to one example in China: One evening, after we had just completed teaching some Chinese servants at a hide- away deserted factory, makeshift training center, several Chinese sisters brought another sister to my room for prayer for healing just before we all retired for the evening. I felt led of the Spirit to use the illustration of Jesus' questions that He sometime asked before ministering healing as well as the James 5 passage as a basis of this hands-on teaching opportunity. We spent time in prayer together and I encouraged them to all participate in this healing ministry.

   I first addressed the sister who was sick, and asked her Jesus' questions: "What do you want Jesus to do for you?" and "Do you want to be well?". Then I shared from James 5 concerning whether or not the sister who was ill knew of any sin in her life that might have contributed to her illness. I was expecting her to say that there was not, but to my total surprise, she said there was sin in her life that might have caused the sickness! I very cautiously enquired whether she felt the freedom to share with all of us or in privacy. She responded that she needed to confess before us all that she had bitterness and unforgiveness in her heart and that it was an offence toward one of the sisters who had brought her to me for prayer!

So, I dealt first with her unforgiveness and bitterness and she confessed this to the Lord and received His forgiveness and cleansing. Then I addressed the sisters who had brought her to me to search their hearts to know which one of them was the offender? We waited on the Spirit to minister for several minutes before the guilty sister began weeping and fell at the feet of the offended sister, begging forgiveness. The two sisters reconciled their relationship and we all laid hands on and anointed with oil the sister who was ill and she was gloriously healed and all glory went to our Lord!

There are many other life illustrations I could share, Don, but this will suffice for the time being.

Love and blessings,

Dan

The Prayer of Relinquishment

Catherine Marshall[1]

When I first began active experimentation with prayer, I was full of questions such as: why are some agonizingly sincere prayers granted, while others are not? Today I still have questions. Mysteries about prayer are always ahead of knowledge – luring, beckoning on to further experimentation.

But one thing I do know; I learned it through hard experience. It's a way of prayer that has resulted consistently in a glorious answer because each time, power beyond human reckoning has been released. This is the prayer of relinquishment.

I got my first glimpse of it in 1943. I had then been ill for six months with a widespread lung infection, and

---

1 *Breakthrough International Ministry of Intercessory Prayer* was started in 1980 by well known Christian author Catherine Marshall and her husband, Leonard LeSourd. Catherine was married to United States Senate Chaplain Peter Marshall when his sudden death in 1949 from a heart attack propelled her into a writing career. Her best selling book titled *A Man Called Peter* was made into the top grossing motion picture of the year in 1952. Many subsequent books were also best sellers, including *Christy*, which later became the popular television series by the same name.

a bevy of specialists seemed unable to help. Persistent prayer, using all the faith I could muster, had resulted in – nothing.

One afternoon, a pamphlet was put in my hands. It was the story of a missionary who had been invalid for eight years. Constantly, she had prayed that God would make her well, so that she might do His work. Finally, worn out with futile petition, she prayed, "All right, I give up. If You want me to be an invalid, that's Your business. I want You even more than I want health. You decide." Within two weeks, the woman was out of bed, completely well. This made no sense to me, yet I could not forget the story. On the morning of September 14 – how can I ever forget the date? I came to the same point of abject acceptance. "I'm tired of asking," was the burden of my prayer. "I'm beaten, finished. God, You decide what You want for me."

Tears flowed. I felt no faith as I understood faith, expected nothing.

And the result? It was as if I had touched a button that opened windows in heaven; as if some dynamo of heavenly power began flowing, flowing. Within a few hours, I had experienced the presence of the Living Christ in a way that wiped away all doubt and revolutionized my life. From that moment, my recovery began.

Through this incident, God was trying to teach me something important about prayer. Gradually, I saw that a demanding spirit, with self-will as its rudder, blocks prayer. I understood that the reason for this is that God absolutely refuses to violate our free will; unless self-will is voluntarily given up, even God cannot move to answer prayer.

Jesus' prayer in the Garden of Gethsemane is this pattern for us. Christ could have avoided the Cross. He did not have to go up to Jerusalem the last time. He could have compromised with the priests, bargained with Caiaphas. He could have capitalized on His following and appeased Judas by setting up the beginning of an earthly Kingdom. Pilate wanted to release Him, all but begged Him to say the right words that would let him do so. Even in the Garden on the night of the betrayal, He had plenty of time and opportunity to flee. Instead, Christ used His free will to turn the decision over to His Father.

The Phillips translation of the Gospels brings Jesus' prayer into special focus: "Dear Father... all things are possible to You. Let me not have to drink this cup! Yet it is not what I want, but what You want." The prayer was not answered as the human Jesus wished. Yet power has been flowing from His Cross ever since. Even at the moment when Christ was bowing to the possibility of an awful death by crucifixion, He never forgot either the presence or the power of God.

There is a crucial difference here between acceptance and resignation. There is no resignation in the prayer of relinquishment. Resignation says, "This is my situation, and I resign myself and settle down to it." Resignation lies down in the dust of a godless universe and steels itself for the worst.

Acceptance says, "True, this is my situation at the moment. I'll look unblinkingly at the reality of it. But, I'll also open up my hands to accept willingly whatever a loving Father sends." Thus acceptance never slams the door on hope.

Yet, even while it hopes, our relinquishment must be the real thing – and this giving up of self-will is the hardest thing we human beings are ever called to do. It's good to remember that not even the Master Shepherd can lead if the sheep do not follow Him. That's the why of Christ's insistence of a very practical obedience: *And why call ye Me, Lord, Lord, and do not the things which I say?* Obey... obedience ... trust... is all over the Gospels. The pliability of an obedient heart must be complete from the set of our wills right on through our actions.

So we take the first hard steps of obedience. And lo, as we stop hiding our eyes, force ourselves to walk up to the fear and look it full in the face – never forgetting that God and His power are still the supreme reality – the fear evaporates. Drastic? Yes. But it is one sure way of releasing prayer power into human affairs.

In the prayer of faith, our hand is still in His. Our heart is still obedient. But now, He has led us out of the frightening darkness, with only the pressure of His hand to reassure us, into the sunlight. We look into the face beside us with a thrill of recognition – the hand of the Father is Jesus' hand!

All along, our heart told us it was so.

Relinquishment? Faith? Just daring to trust Jesus.

Father, for such a long time I have pleaded before You this, the deep desire of my heart:______.

Yet, the more I have clamored for Your help with this, the more remote You have seemed.

I confess my demanding spirit in this matter. I've tried suggesting to You ways my prayer could be answered. To my shame, I have even bargained with You. Yet I know that trying to manipulate the Lord of the Universe is utter foolishness.

I want to trust You, Father. My spirit knows that these verities are forever trustworthy even when I feel nothing.

That You are there

That You love me

That You alone know what is best for me

Perhaps all along, You have been waiting for me to give up self-effort. At last, I want You in my life even more than I want ________. So now, by an act of my will, I relinquish this to You. I will accept Your will, whatever that may be. Thank You for counting this act of my will as a decision of the real person even when my emotions protest.

I ask You to hold me true to this decision. To You, Lord God, who alone are worthy of worship, I bend the knee with thanksgiving that this too will work together for my good. I relinquish this to You.

Amen

Other Books Available at

www.DonAtkin.com

Like Father, Like Son

Royal Priesthood,
The Pathway to Kingdom Authority

Groundswell

Church and Kingdom – Here and Now

Identity Theft

God's Glorious Government

Nothing Else Really Matters

Sons of the Kingdom

Creation's Cry

A Desperate World
In the Hands of a New Creation

Acts of a New Creation

All are also available in Kindle and ePub versions!

Made in the USA
Middletown, DE
30 January 2023